DANIEL BOONE

THE PIONEER OF KENTUCKY

A Biography.

BY

GEORGE CANNING HILL

Patrick Henry University Press
Colorado Springs, Colorado

Daniel Boone:
The Pioneer of Kentucky

by
George Canning Hill

ISBN: 1-4101-0092-8

Copyright © 2002 by Fredonia Books

Reprinted from the 1890 edition

Patrick Henry University Press
An Imprint of Fredonia Books
Colorado Springs, Colorado
http://www.patrickhenryuniversitypress.com

All rights reserved, including the right to reproduce this book, or portions thereof, in any form.

In order to make original editions of historical works available to scholars at an economical price, this facsimile of the original edition of 1890 is reproduced from the best available copy and has been digitally enhanced to improve legibility, but the text remains unaltered to retain historical authenticity.

PREFACE.

The author has designed the present series of Biographies more particularly for the young. And in pursuing his original plan along to its termination, he has set before himself the following objects, to which he invites the reader's attention:

To furnish from the pages of the world's history a few examples of true manhood, lofty purpose, and persevering effort, such as may be safely held up either for the admiration or emulation of the youth of the present day;

To clear away, in his treatment of these subjects, whatever mistiness and mustiness may have accumulated with time about them, presenting to the mental vision fresh and living pictures, that shall seem to be clothed with naturalness, and energy, and vitality;

To offer no less instruction to the minds, than pleasure to the imaginations of the many for whom he has taken it in hand to write;

And, more especially, perhaps, to familiarize the youth

of our day with those striking and manly characters, that have long ago made their mark, deep and lasting, on the history and fortunes of the AMERICAN CONTINENT.

The deeds of these men, it is true, are to be found abundantly recorded in Histories; but they lie so scattered along their ten thousand pages, and are so intermixed with the voluminous records of other matters, as to be practically out of the reach of the *younger* portion of readers, and so of the very ones for whom this series has been undertaken. These want only *pictures of actual life;* and, if the author shall, in any due degree, succeed even in sketching interesting *outlines*, he will feel that he is answering the very purpose that has long lain unperformed within his heart.

CONTENTS.

CHAPTER I.
HIS EARLY DAYS, ... 9

CHAPTER II.
REMOVAL TO NORTH CAROLINA, ... 27

CHAPTER III.
HIS EMIGRATION TO KENTUCKY, ... 43

CHAPTER IV.
ALL ALONE, ... 63

CHAPTER V.
TRANSYLVANIA, ... 81

CHAPTER VI.
TROUBLE WITH THE INDIANS, ... 104

CHAPTER VII.
BATTLES AND SIEGES, ... 122

CHAPTER VIII.
A PRISONER, ... 141

CHAPTER IX.
A WONDERFUL ESCAPE, ... 160

CHAPTER X.
SIEGE OF BOONESBOROUGH, ... 175

CHAPTER XI.
MISFORTUNES AND TRIALS, ... 192

CHAPTER XII.
LAND AND LAND-OWNING, ... 212

CHAPTER XIII.
A NEW HOME IN THE FAR WEST, . . . 231

CHAPTER XIV.
LAST DAYS OF THE HUNTER. 249

DANIEL BOONE.

CHAPTER I.

HIS EARLY DAYS.

LIFE in the woods is a romance from beginning to end. The mind delights to dwell upon the freedom, the beauty, the trials, and even the hazards of such a life, and thinks of it, in contrast with the set forms and customs of civilization, as something so fresh that it raises the imagination to a pitch of the most pleasurable excitement.

There are very few boys who have not, at one time or another in their lives, felt the secret but strong impulse to go to sea, or to play at a game of Selkirk solitude in the woods. Daniel Webster used to say to his friends when assembled on his lawn at Marshfield, in the summer evenings, that the two objects in creation which chiefly inspired sentiments of grandeur within his breast, were the stars and the sea; he might well have added to these, the forest, than which, in its remote and awful solitudes, nothing in all the world can be named which so imposes lofty and solemn thoughts upon the soul.

We all love nature so much, even those of us who were never nursed upon her bosom. We love the streams, the lawns, the rocks, the trees, the dense masses of foliage, and even the driving snows and deluging rains. That love is born with us; and we cannot altogether outroot it, if we would. The birds and beasts; the grove and river; mountain and waterfall; blue sky and black cloud freighted with thunder; sunsets and sunrisings; the winds that roar and howl themselves hoarse in winter, and the balmy breezes that blow up through the open windows of the south in summer; every one of these is able to strike a chord of sympathy in the human breast, and waken the heart to a living ecstasy.

There have been many men in the world who loved the silence and solitudes of nature, but none, certainly, who pursued the enjoyments they offer with such singleness of heart as the famous Daniel Boone, the pioneer of Kentucky. He was a marked man from the start. Such true and simple children of nature are so rare as to attract a great deal of attention on all sides. Their speech is not the speech of the world; their manners are not those of common men; and their lives are crowded with deeds of daring, whose narration forms the most attractive of romances. Old and young delight to read of the wonderful encounters with Indians and wild beasts; the narrow escape from the perils of flood and forest; the hardy and prolonged endurance, and the steady perseverance and resolution. These are stories of which the young, especially, never tire. They are fresh forever.

It requires peculiar qualities to make a good pioneer. We who enjoy what a heroic ancestry won for us by their own sufferings and sacrifices, know little, and think less, of the cost at which all these things were secured. Some of those noble men marched forth to beat down oppression, as it sought to draw its bands closer and closer around them; and some silently went out into the wilderness, resolved to subdue even nature herself to their far-reaching purposes. But large as was their comprehension, they could not then take into their vision the half of the grand picture which was so soon to unroll, like a panorama, before the gaze of an astonished world.

The name of Daniel Boone, as one of the pio

neers, has gone around the world. Long ago it was celebrated wherever men admired courage, or loved to read stories of individual sacrifice and daring. Captain Cook had sailed around the globe, bringing home with him accounts of men that were known scarcely in the popular imagination; Ledyard traversed wild wastes where vegetation never grew, and made himself famous for the courage he displayed in penetrating to climes that were thought unable to sustain human life; but Boone set out with calmness, as if he were obeying a religious inspiration, and buried himself forever in the wilderness. It required great resolution to do what he did; and yet it seemed to come to him as easily as play to a child.

Lord Byron proclaimed his undying fame in some of his noblest verse, which deserves to be incorporated with a biographical sketch of the man. It is as follows:

> "Of all men, saving Sylla, the man-slayer,
>   Who passes for, in life and death, most lucky,
> Of the great names which in our faces stare,
>   The General Boone, backwoodsman, of Kentucky,
> Was happiest among mortals anywhere;
>   For, killing nothing but a bear or buck, he
> Enjoyed the lonely, vigorous, harmless days
> Of his old age, in wilds of deepest maze.

"Crime came not near him— she is not the child
    Of solitude ; health shrank not from him — for
Her home is in the rarely trodden wild,
    Where, if men seek her not, and death be more
Their choice than life, forgive them, as, beguiled
    By habit, to what their own hearts abhor,
In cities caged. The present case in point I
Cite is, that Boone lived hunting up to ninety;

"And what's still stranger, left behind a name
    For which men vainly decimate the throng;
Not only famous, but of that good fame,
    Without which, glory's but a tavern song—
Simple, serene, the antipodes of shame,
    Which hate nor envy e'er could tinge with wrong;
An active hermit, even in age the child
Of nature, or the man of Ross run wild.

"'Tis true he shrank from men even of his nation.
    When they built up into his darling trees,
He moved some hundred miles off, for a station
    Where there were fewer houses, and more ease.
The inconvenience of civilization
    Is, that you neither can be pleased, nor please.
But where he met the individual man,
He showed himself as kind as mortal can.

"He was not all alone; around him grew
    A sylvan tribe of children of the chase,
Whose young, unwaken'd world was ever new;
    Nor sword nor sorrow yet had left a trace
On her unwrinkled brow, nor could you view
    A frown on nature's, or on human face ;
The free-born forest found and kept them free,
And fresh as is a torrent or a tree.

"And tall, and strong, and swift of foot were they,
    Beyond the dwarfing city's pale abortions ;
Because their thoughts had never been the prey
    Of care or gain; the green woods were their portions.

No sinking spirits told them they grew grey;
   No fashion made them apes of her distortions.
Simple they were, not savage; and their rifles,
   Though very true, were not yet used for trifles.

"Motion was in their days, rest in their slumbers,
   And cheerfulness the handmaid of their toil;
Nor yet too many nor too few their numbers;
   Corruption could not make their hearts her soil.
The lust which stings, the splendor which encumbers,
   With the free foresters divide no spoil.
Serene, not sullen, were the solitudes
Of this unsighing people of the woods."

It is to be remembered, too, that when Boone shouldered his rifle and went with his little family into the wilderness, the days of the American Revolution were just drawing nigh. Had he listened intently, it would seem as if he could have almost caught the echoes of the early cannon fired by his resisting countrymen, and heard the roll of the drums, and the tramp of the ill-clad armies that were mustering in the field. But as his life chanced to be cast without the immediate reach of these influences, nothing was left him but to follow the direction of his own tastes or desires. He loved the mysteries of woodcraft; he yearned for the companionship that silence alone offered him; he sighed daily, even at the season of early manhood, for the unbroken delights of solitude; and by all these signs had God sent him into the world to be a pioneer. Any other life would have been a mistake for him.

We are all over apt to consider only those men the real founders of our nation, who perilled their lives or fortunes in the strife of the Revolution; but we allow ourselves to rest much short of the reality, when we do so. A great share of that work was done in silence and solitude; by self-sacrifices that were not seen by the eyes of the world — not in the smoke and roar of battle, but with patient and repeated efforts — frequently offering scarce a hope of final success. The men who lived and labored thus, were at least equal heroes with any other. They endured as much; they toiled as much; they made as noble sacrifices for their posterity; and the results that flowed, and still flow, out of their endeavor, are no wise behind what has been wrought by the rest, either in importance or permanence.

The true way to look at the claims of the different workers for the inheritance we now enjoy, is to regard them, one and all, as engaged in the selfsame purpose; to study them as the individuals of a fraternity; to match what one accomplished in one place and direction, with what another accomplished in an opposite or corresponding one. They labored together in a body, shoulder to shoulder, though perhaps they knew it not at the time, nor even knew what great things they were doing. Each one took the part which heaven had allotted him, and worked it out as far as time and strength permitted.

And out of the long and brilliant list of patriots — whether orators, or warriors, or statesmen, or divines, whether at work in this field or that — no name shines with a purer or steadier lustre than that of Daniel Boone. Even for the days in which he lived, he was accounted a wonderful being; and those who read or heard of him felt the bewitching influence of his very name. No boy ever hung over the fictitious narrative of Alexander Selkirk with any greater delight and wonder, than did the men and women of the days following the Revolution over the real story of Boone and his romantic fortunes in the great Western wilderness. Stories of his courage and fortitude came to the ears of his countrymen on the seaboard, like whispering voices out of the pathless woods; and all alike were enchanted. It was so new, so fresh, so strange, this life away from the reach of civilization; the imagination loved to go out into just such realms as those in which he dwelt, and to people them in obedience to its own laws alone.

The Boone family sprang from English soil, and

once dwelt in pleasant Devonshire, that spot of earth whose rich slopes and emerald pasture-lands are the glory of the mother country, and accounted among the garden-spots of the globe. The ancestor who brought the name to America, was George Boone. He came with his bounteous family of nineteen children (nine sons and ten daughters), and settled on the broad acres that lay open for his possession in Berks County, Pennsylvania. This George Boone, it seems, had a great ambition to hold land, and in time became the owner of noble tracts, not only in the county where he settled, but likewise in the adjoining States of Maryland and Virginia.

England had not land enough for his great needs —that is, land that he might, by his own effort and industry, acquire. In America there was plenty for all, and uncounted acres to spare. It was in the year 1717, that George Boone came over to this country, and at a time when the people of overcrowded England began seriously to turn their attention to the advantages offered them on this unpeopled soil.

George Boone was, of course, a patriarch, with such a long roll of children, and deserves to be held in honor as the respected head of so large a family. He came out to see the land, and possess it. Having exhausted the vocabulary of scripture-titles in naming his children, as the custom was in those times, he gave the odd name of "Squire" to the one who otherwise might have gone without any. This Squire Boone, when he came to manhood, married a young woman named Morgan, and settled in Bucks County, in Pennsylvania. Of course, he was not far away from his father.

He raised up a large family also, as his father had done before him. He named his sons Samuel, and Israel, and Daniel, and Jonathan, and when he came to the seventh and last, he saw no other way than to give him his own title — Squire.

Daniel Boone was born in Bucks County, in the year 1735, on the 11th of February, and was consequently a little younger than Washington, at the time of the Revolution. He was a boy of a remarkably good constitution, which was about the best inheritance his parents could leave him. At three years of age he was removed, with the family, into what is now the town of Reading, Berks County — then, however, but a meagre and exposed post on the outskirts of the wilderness. The Indians threatened the peace of the settlement at all hours. It was not safe to go out of the reach of the dwelling, unless precautions were taken against sudden attacks from the forest natives. Ambushes were likely to be sprung upon the settlers on every side.

It was in a school of danger like this that the boy, then scarcely more than an infant, received his first lessons in life; and it may be believed they were rugged and lasting ones. Here on the edge of the trackless forest, his pliant mind was impressed with those images of nature, and those pictures of the pleasures of solitude, which are very apt to be indelible. He played about the far-off settlement, and gazed into the scowling wilderness with feelings that, during all his subsequent life, he labored to make real and true.

There he learned all about the tricks and traits of the Indians. The talk was chiefly upon them and their wily habits. He learned the dangers of the life his parents led, and was, at the same time, taught to love perfect simplicity. He was taught, too, that peacefulness brought the most happiness, agreeably to the views of his parents and those around him.

During his seclusion in the woods, it is not to be supposed that he enjoyed quite as many privileges as young lads do in these days, especially in the way of schooling. His education was very limited and meagre. Schooling did not mean then as much as it does now. Then, it was but a hard chance indeed. The books were few, and teachers were rare. Little more than the rudiments were taught, and taught very hastily at that. The scholars did not assemble in fine buildings, and seat themselves at handsome desks, as they do now; but were compelled to huddle together as best they could in close and ill-lighted log cabins, the rudest structures that can be conceived.

The sturdy men of those times were educated in a rough school. It was almost a necessity that they should be. They knew much less of books than they did of life. They stammered over their spelling, perhaps, but made it up in their action. Polish was not much wanted then, but rather ruggedness and strength.

We can, in imagination, look into one of these log huts on the Pennsylvania frontier, now, and see the little lad Boone, busy over his tasks. Simple enough they were, yet no doubt as difficult for him to master as the incomparably tougher ones that are set before the boys of the present day. We can behold him gazing intently out through the open window, which, in fact, is no more than a square hole in the side of the cabin, and roaming, in thought, among the dense and dark trees, all among the mysterious shadows, or into and out of the recesses, that hide nowhere as they can in the forest. He, no doubt, sat, as many an impatient schoolboy has sat on his bench since, and dreamed of what was just beyond his reach outside — of butterflies, and green grass, and running across meadows, with no teacher to watch them, and freedom from restraint of every character. He would have been very different from other boys if he had not done so.

Of course, he was glad to get through the routine of school, and have it done with forever. The day of his release from that unwilling service, he considered as the most to be desired of any in his life. He learned to read, to write, and to cipher; these were all. And it cannot be asserted that he was anything beyond perfection in any of these. He did not pretend to write with more accuracy or elegance than the other boys of his time. Nor were his exploits in the way of spelling very much to be boasted of. He was a good reader, no doubt, as those things then went. And perhaps when we have said this much about the early schooling of Daniel Boone, we have said all.

As his life was to be in the woods, he looked at no education except that which would give him skill and advantage there. The books could have taught him not the first syllable of the sort of learning he most wanted. That he could better acquire of the Indians, of the elements, of the open day, and the mysterious night, of the very animals that made their abode in the wilderness. The seasons themselves became his instructors. Nature was a volume always open to him; and he studied it with eagerness and devotion.

The forest, too, was thought to be the scene of many and many a contest between the white man and the Indian. Hence the character of the savage was studied with the greatest care and patience. If the woods were indeed his special hunting-ground, and it was not permitted the white man to roam over them also, it would not be a great while before the reason for the latter's exclusion was better understood. And in order to meet the savage on an equal footing, it was necessary for the former to understand his nature at every crook and turn.

Nobody could tell, easier than the Indian, the paths that conducted them through the tangled forest mazes. He was an expert in arts like this. And it was exactly such as this that the frontier settler had to learn of him, enemy as he was, in order to be anywhere near his equal. How to make his escape in time of imminent danger, was a problem which it required a good deal of study and skillful practise to solve. How to match his savage rival in the thousand arts and dissimulations that he was so ready to practise, was quite enough to occupy all his time and thought.

Young Boone grew up in the midst of circumstances and influences like these. Whatever else he did not learn, he certainly did learn the most lasting lessons of self-reliance. Here was he strong; and here was his strength always to lie. He felt the peculiar glory there was in trusting to himself, in relying on his own exertions. No school could have been a better one, either, to teach him how to make the most of what means lay around him; how to keep himself always on his feet; how to extricate himself from any kind of difficulties that threatened to hem him in; and how to perform the most with the fewest means, and under the greatest discouragements.

Of course he learned to use the gun as soon as he had the strength to carry it about with him. He became an expert marksman very early. Sharp shooting, in fact, was necessary almost to his existence; and if not so much so at the time, it certainly became so in more than a single instance afterwards. As he grew up nearer to the limit of manhood, his love of hunting and solitude became more and more noticeable. He would be off alone in the woods, with nothing but his gun for company, all through the day. Many a story is told of his wonderful feats, such as the number of animals he brought down with his unerring bullet, or the fierce and finally successful encounters he was wont to have with the forest denizens. The whole settlement looked upon him with pride, if not with hope; for they saw in him those shining qualities that give lasting fame to the frontiersman and pioneer.

Having acquired the fame of a hunter, it was natural enough that he should think of no other occupation in life. So he soon began to grow restless under the restraints of home, and finally went out from beneath his father's roof and built a little hut in the forest, where he played the hermit and woodsman to his heart's content. The wild beasts roamed all around him by day, and their howlings made a dismal concert for him at night. He was alone; yet the solitude never became oppressive to him. He had yearned for just such a life since he began to estimate what life was worth.

The walls of his hut were hung around with skins of animals, trophies of his skill and daring. He stood in the door of his rude cabin of logs, and contemplated the forest, with its profound silence and gloom, with a pleasure that none could understand. In the untrodden depths of that wilderness he tried, no doubt, to find his own future; which, even then, he felt was as full of mazy windings and dark recesses, as the forest itself. He tried, in short, to taste the life he so much longed for, in advance of its coming; he sought to make his fancies real as fast as he could, impatient that time did not untie the pack at its back a little faster.

CHAPTER II.

REMOVAL TO NORTH CAROLINA.

SQUIRE Boone, the father of Daniel, made up his mind after a time to remove with his family to a tract in North Carolina. He had been off on a visit among his friends in Maryland; and it was while there, that he first heard the alluring stories of the land in North Carolina, which made him uneasy in remaining longer where he was. He remembered, too, the large family on his hands, and how necessary it was to make provision in the future for them. He must have land enough to settle all his boys upon around him, and they would very soon be men. In Pennsylvania, he had a fear that ere long he would be crowded; but in North Carolina the land was taken up by fewer settlers, and he thought he could more easily secure what he wanted.

Daniel was no doubt glad to go. He had grown familiar with all the scenes about his Pennsylvania home, and would be delighted to start off and try nature in another region. This change of location, too, taking him as it did into still more remote solitudes, was just the school for the work he had yet to do. The boy had now reached the age of eighteen years, almost manhood; but he was the fresh child of nature still.

After the usual busy preparations, the family set out from Reading on their long and lonely journey, through Maryland and Virginia, for North Carolina. It was a sad scene, the parting with the friends and neighbors, those with whom the Boones had shared a common danger in the wilderness. They felt that they were cutting loose from all they held dear in life, and were going forth again, as it were, to open a path for themselves in the world. We can see that little band of a single family starting off into the wilderness; the father walking now at the head of the line, and now in the rear, keeping watch against surprises, and overseeing the details of the march; the mother and her younger children safely stowed in the tented wagon, whose snow-white top showed far off as it receded in the depths of the forest; young Daniel, with his rifle across his shoulder — tall, straight and manly in his appearance, noting the signs of the season everywhere around him, with an eye awake to any enemy that might be near, and wondering and dreaming, perhaps, of his untried future.

Little is known, however, of the particulars of that most important journey. If its details could all be told, they would form a chapter that every man, woman, and child in America would be eager to read. But unfortunately the story is not preserved; and we of this day are left to imagine what it really was. We know at least that it was crowded with trials and deprivations, and that even in the brave heart of the father there were moments when doubt and fear had their way. Yet he pushed on, and finally reached in safety the promised land.

The first thing he did was to select a spot near a stream. This river was called the South Yadkin. It rises in the northwestern part of North Carolina, in the mountain country, runs across the State in a southeasterly course, thence through a corner of South Carolina, and pours itself into the Atlantic above the mouth of the Santee. When he settled down near this river, it was the year 1753; a little more than a century ago.

Here young Daniel Boone lived with his father's family, and here he arrived at full manhood. His life differed not much from that which he led in Pennsylvania. He practised with his rifle; he made constant excursions all around the family settlement; he increased his capacity for self-reliance; he continually tried his courage; he learned more minutely than ever the silent laws of forest life, and what a close relation they had to his fortunes and his nature.

About this time, too, great events were transpiring in the world, and grander ones were preparing. The French and English were at war with each other, and the contest was transferred to this continent, where it was waged with terrific fury. It was along through these years that Israel Putnam was getting his valuable experience as a soldier in the neighborhood of Lake George, fighting bravely against the French and Indians. Washington, too, was schooling under Braddock in the Western wilderness, having already acquired the quick eye and the firm foot, in his perilous enterprises as a surveyor in the depths of the forest. But the war was not felt as far as among the mountains in the neighborhood of the South Yadkin. There the few settlers dwelt in peace, scarcely touched by the wave of battle that broke and died before its roar sounded in their ears.

Peaceful and quiet was the life of the young pioneer, himself ignorant of what the future had in store. He was, with his father, a plain and hard-working farmer, helping the best he could to clear the land and get it ready for cultivation. This labor he relieved with hunting, losing none of the skill he had already acquired with the rifle. In this double capacity of farmer and hunter, the years wore noiselessly away. The country about him began to fill up, from time to time, with new settlers. Families came from a long distance to occupy the land which had so much promise for them. The forests began to melt before the invading axe, that heralds the march of civilization. Settlers' cabins were to be seen here and there, over the wide landscape. The crack of the hunter's rifle was to be heard more frequently in all directions. Farms were opening to the light of day, and beginning to bless their owners with the earth's bounteous increase.

Among the families that came and settled near the Yadkin, and in the immediate neighborhood of the Boones, was one by the name of Bryan; a name at this day held in honor in the State of North Carolina. The Boones and the Bryans were not long in finding the secret pleasures that belong to friendship and good neighborhood. Like many other families that share the burdens of distance and solitude, they soon became intimate. Among the Bryans was a young girl, a daughter, named Rebecca; and for her young Daniel Boone soon found he felt an ardent attachment. It was, in fact, the first dawning of love.

He was fonder of the forest, he had thought hitherto, than of any human society, and he knew that this love was growing stronger in his heart every day, too; yet there was a stronger attraction about this young girl, Rebecca Bryan, than he could find even in the charms of forest life. He knew not what it was. He had never been in love before, and, in fact, had never thought of such a thing. But now, of a sudden, he discovered that all his life had taken a new coloring, and his hopes and feelings were fast centering on an object, whose power to attract one like himself he had never dreamed of. It is a very common thing for a young man to fall in love; and Daniel Boone, at his time of life, was no exception to the great rule.

A pretty story is told of an accident which came very near occurring, while he was paying attention to young Rebecca Bryan; but whether it is quite true or not, is a matter of some doubt. It is said that, while out hunting deer one day, he observed a pair of bright eyes looking steadily at him from out the thicket. He raised his rifle to his shoulder, and was on the point of firing, when a timely movement on the part of the *owner* of the eyes disclosed to him the fact that he had come very near shooting his intended bride!

Soon after the acquaintance between these two young persons ripened into intimacy and love, they were married. This was Daniel Boone's first real step out into the world; for now he left the roof of his father, and set up housekeeping for himself. Now he was an independent man, the head of a family of his own. He had his own living to earn; he must now hunt and farm for the support of her whom he had taken to wife; they both had left father and mother, sister and brother, and gone off to dwell apart by themselves. Of course, it was a sudden turn in the fortunes of both of them.

Before he married, however, he tramped a long distance up the valley of the Yadkin River, desirous of finding a spot on which to locate. He wanted to be off again. He did not like the settlements any better than he used to in Pennsylvania. Solitude was still his strong desire. The valley led away in the direction of the mountains, where the forest still stood untamed. The nearer he got to them, the more serene became his heart. There he felt sure he should find the peace for which he yearned.

At length he pitched upon a proper place, and erected his little cabin. It was a rude structure, all of logs. Into this cabin he was to take his bride. The frowning shadows from the mountains beyond, lay across his very door. He could sit and study the play of the lightnings along their sides at evening, yet feel perfectly secure in his lonely home. The wild beasts set up their nightly cries around him. The little stream flowed by as silently as if it were dreaming, and did not wish to have its dreams broken. Dense and dark was the forest, on the right hand and the left. The morning sun came and filled the valley with its ever new glory; and at evening its golden arrows lodged in the tops of the giant trees, and its dying play gave new features to the landscape. No one came in at the door all day; and at night the solitude remained still unbroken. They feared the intrusion of no stranger. They were in a world of their own. Sky and trees hemmed them in, and were welcome boundaries to these children of nature. He knew how to read the secrets of the forest, for in the forest he had obtained all his schooling; and no student of books and black-letter was ever more wrapped in the delights of his avocation. Upon no human face did his eyes rest during all this time, save the face of his youthful wife; their sympathies must have been made a thousand times more quick and deep, by the steady pressure of the surrounding silence and solitude. He found companionship in the animals, whose habits he was obliged to study; in the countless varieties of life, animate and inanimate, around him; in the song of wild birds by day, and the howl of bears, and wolves, and panthers, by night; in the ripple of streams, the blowing of winds, the roar of the lofty tree-tops; in grass, and flowers, and sunshine; in clouds, and rain, and storms; and, beyond all these, in the fathomless deep of his own soul.

We have no detailed account of his way of life, after he took his young wife off into the wilderness to clear up a little settlement of their own. It must have been monotonous to most persons, though to one whose whole being had been tutored only in the solitudes of nature, it was, undoubtedly, full of variety and freshness, and new daily experiences. So great a difference is there in the modes of education. If we had the facts of this part of his life to present, no romance of woodcraft could offer rarer attractions to the youthful or the mature reader; but imagination is left to supply for itself the lack which all alike deplore. It is unfortunate that the best and bravest men are at such slight pains to hand along the story of their career; yet, like the real children of nature they are, they think no more of being brave and great, than others do of being cowardly and mean; and it is a prominent trait of nobility, that it is ever forgetful of self, and satisfied with merely doing its work.

His cabin was the only one, for a long time, in that part of the Yadkin Valley. His firelight blazed in the eye of no other man's firelight. No door faced his door. No man's possessions joined his possessions. He lived a forest monarch, brave, self-reliant, and strong. But time, with its changes, was all ready to crowd him along. Hitherto he had only been in training for the future in which he was to play so large a part; now he was to be forced to step forward into that future, and, by his very courage in taking that step, to show that his was the spirit which the coming time chiefly needed. Other settlers came straggling along, with their families, into his neighborhood, invited by the richness of the lands and the beauty of the scenery. Soon he saw himself surrounded, and the smokes of other cabins going up in all directions about that of his own. He felt himself hedged in. It did not suit him to know that somebody's lands adjoined his lands, or that he was not free to hunt and farm as far as his eye could reach and his feet carry him. The same oppression that his father had felt before him, when he made up his mind to remove from Pennsylvania, determined him to leave the place to which so many others were now flocking. Others might be thankful for human society; young Boone was not: the hermit nature was even now fully developed within him.

This feature, in fact, was the great peculiarity of Daniel Boone — his dislike of society, and his passion for utter solitude. He felt himself growing stronger in proportion to the growth of this love of loneliness. Other men seek to prop themselves up by surrounding themselves with social advantages; they swim with the aid of corks and floats: but Boone at an early age found out a better secret than this; he learned that power was born out of one's own self, and that if a man was first his own complete master, he might easily claim like mastery over others around him. And Boone was right. His views would tend to make men simple and true in their relations to others, and compel them to begin and end all their efforts with themselves. As it is now, the strife is to achieve conquests over others, before we practise anything of the kind upon ourselves.

The pleasant Yadkin banks were to be deserted

at length, and new projects of adventure to be undertaken. Henceforward there was to be no rest by the way; it was to be a history of unceasing toil, and travel, and trial, and solitude. He only felt the desire for solitude controlling him; he did not know to what vast results it was going to lead. There was a wild and unexplored land beyond the western mountains, of which he had heard strange stories, but upon which no white man had as yet ventured to set foot. Thither his thoughts directed themselves. Somewhere within that unknown expanse of territory, he secretly felt that he could erect his cabin, and live forever undisturbed. There were highly colored reports abroad respecting the scenery of that virgin country; the mountains were matchless for grandeur; the plains stretched out before the eye like magnificent pictures; the streams were gigantic and lordly, draining thousands of square miles in their winding courses; and the forests stood out against the sky, darker and denser than any even of those lofty growths with which the common mind of the pioneer was perfectly familiar. Columbus did not feel his great imagination more profoundly excited with what he had heard of the passage westward around the world, than did Daniel Boone his, with these wonderful tales of the vast land that lay beyond the mountains.

There were stories, to be sure, of Indians, whose keen eyes pierced the gloom, and whose sagacious feet threaded the depths of those western forests, and it was well enough known that these savages were blood-thirsty and merciless in their nature; yet Boone felt the rising of no fear even at the recital of these. His fertile imagination, and his passionate love of solitude readily overcame all that timidity which would have asserted its control in other men; and the thickening dangers, in fact, only excited him the more to go forth and achieve their mastery. And the very fact that this region was all undescribed — that no white man had set his foot within its borders, that the soil was virgin, the rivers unexplored, the natives unknown, the beasts, and birds, and fishes, all ready for the conquest of him who had the courage and perseverance to undertake it — gave increased zest to his dreamings on the subject and helped to fix and fire his determination. He lived quietly where he then was, and revolved it all in his mind. Being such a complete solitary, he communicated his plans to few or none around him. Each day saw his purpose, at first dim and indistinct, fast taking form and acquiring strength. When he worked on his little cultivated patch, and when he tramped in the woods with his trusty rifle, he was thinking, thinking, thinking, and of nothing but this plan to plunge into the great wilderness of the West, and make his home in the very heart and secrets of nature.

There were other men, too, about this time, who had given the same subject more or less attention; but they did not go about it as Boone did. They believed the wilderness would certainly come to be explored and settled in time, but by no means in their day; it was too great an undertaking, especially by a mere handfull of raw frontier settlers, far removed from the assistance and sympathy of the population along the Atlantic seaboard. No doubt they felt as well assured as Boone did that the mountains to the west would in time be crossed by the lengthening lines of hardy emigrants; but they were only dreaming of somebody else coming forward in the future to accomplish this, while he was thinking of doing it himself. There was, however, this difference in their plans: they were calculating for the advancement of civilization, while he was in the silent search of solitude for himself. It was well, even as it was; for without this very passion for solitude, he would have had no adequate motive to spur him on. The reader can see for himself already, that while the other settlers thought only of the general advantage in the future, he was intently brooding over his own; and it is only through the operation of these strong and personal motives that mankind has been led along to its present condition.

What the conquest of the Rocky Mountains has been in our own day, the victorious passage of the Cumberland Ridge was to the bold pioneers of the days of Daniel Boone. We have the aid of science, of government, and of numbers; and if one wave of progress is not able to surmount such barriers, another is all ready to follow it, that will. There was no help of this sort, however, in those ruder times. Then each man had to rely on his muscular arm, his quick eye, and his unerring aim; if he fell, there was not much hope that others, coming from the settlements that could illy spare them, would very soon follow him; and the tales of peril would, of course, become magnified many fold.

None of the professed hunters of that day were before Boone for courage and daring. He had penetrated farther into the forest than any one else. He was well aware how little it required to sustain human life, away from the haunts of men. In the untrodden forests he knew that he could do without house or shelter, and that his own skill was able to secure him his livelihood. But the greatest object of his fears was the savage. The Carolina settlers had some personal experience with the habits of the red man, who had crept stealthily to the borders of their settlements, and put all things in sudden jeopardy. Boone had no reason to suppose there was less cause to fear him on his own ground than in the neighborhood of the white settlements. The roving Cherokees left dark legends wherever their feet had trod. To push into the wilderness in the face of such savages, swarming on every hand, would seem to be the utmost confession of hardihood itself. We may never know of the many bloody encounters between the white and the red men, just before the great hunter of Kentucky shouldered his rifle and went into the deep solitudes; but imagination pictures to us many a cruel encounter, and many a fiendish surprise of innocent men and women, the record of which sleeps in the same silence with the names of the Indian chieftains themselves.

Judge Marshall says of the country beyond the Cumberland Mountains, that at that time (in 1767), " It appeared to the dusky view of the generality of the people of Virginia, almost as obscure and doubtful as America itself to the people of Europe before the voyage of Columbus. A country there was; of this none could doubt who thought at all; but whether land or water, mountain or plain, fertility or barrenness, preponderated; whether inhabited by men or beasts, or both, or neither, they knew not. If inhabited by men, they were supposed to be Indians; for such had always infested the frontiers. And this had been a powerful reason for not exploring the region west of the great mountain which concealed Kentucky from their sight.

Such was the land that was to be possessed. The man whose mission it was to go out and take possession, working even greater things than he knew at the time, was Daniel Boone. We will proceed now to give a clue to his motives in changing his residence still again, and to portray the character whose simple strength was sufficient for the grand movement of which he was the pioneer.

CHAPTER III.

HIS EMIGRATION TO KENTUCKY.

WHEN white settlers began to increase on the banks of the Yadkin, Boone seriously thought it was time to be off. He had no idea of going as the leader of others, or of handing down his name to future generations. His highest desire was to be rid of the sight or sound of a settlement. Yet although his motive was so wholly centered in self, the elements of his nature were exactly those required for the important work of a pioneer. He had taught himself, from his earliest youth, the valuable lesson of self-reliance. His necessities were few and readily supplied; his habits were simple in the extreme; while he was at heart as gentle as a girl, he concealed beneath that gentleness the courage and boldness of a lion; he would avoid danger as long as he could; but when no other course was left him, he could stand by and defend as long as any man living. He was peaceful, therefore, and loved solitude more than society. And when he saw the society he cared not for creeping slowly up to the very verge of the untamed wilderness, he thought it was high time to take his departure.

It is important for the reader to remember that none of the common vices of the pioneer found lodgement in the pure and simple nature of Daniel Boone. He was as conscientious and true, as he was brave and bold; and he probably loved the solitudes of nature the more, because he disliked contact with the vices and follies of men. Boone was no common pioneer. He was the man for the time, and his nature had been kept sweet and clean for the work to which he was called. There is no influence like that of solitude to protect the heart from contamination. He shunned society because he was not satisfied with what it gave him. It was superficial and shallow, while he was sincere and true. And yet no man was of a more kind and peaceful disposition, or better inclined to do generous deeds for others. But the artificialities of social life had no attraction for him. He saw that it was expected of all who belonged to the social brotherhood, to adopt certain forms that others were to set up, and copy certain customs and habits that others were to establish for him; and in his view there was no good reason why he was not quite as well able to lay down rules for himself, as other men were to do so for him. It would be ridiculous to think of making a man of fashion out of a man like Daniel Boone. His was too large and simple a nature to be strapped and cramped within the limits of any such strait-jacket as that. Hence he put all such trifling at once behind his back.

There were other things that helped his determination to leave the frontier and plunge into the wilderness. The officers of the colonial government were altogether too aristocratic in their modes of living, and introduced habits among the thrifty and well-to-do people of the settlement, such as a simple nature like that of Boone could not patiently endure. Grievances also presented themselves, proceeding from the exactions of these officers, who resolved to use their power over the colonists to increase their own personal wealth; and hence taxes, and fees, and costs accumulated so fast that sagacious minds began to grow timid, and to wonder where such practises would end. To escape these things, Boone determined to turn his back on the colony. He was not ready to be bled for the enrichment of lawyers and crown officers of every grade — men who had come among the colonists for the sole purpose of making or mending their fortunes. If his little property was to be eaten up, he would rather it should take the risk of instantaneous destruction at the hands of the savage, than be filtered away, little by little, through the nests of sieves held for it by tax collectors, officers of the law, grabbing speculators, and men of the like character.

The people petitioned the crown for protection against these rapidly multiplying acts of injustice; and their petitions resulted only in the acts becoming multiplied. All through the thirteen American Colonies, at that time, the discussions were warm and frequent whether the mother country had the right to tax at all, unless representation went along with taxation; and in North Carolina the inhabitants were as much aroused to repel the injustice from which they suffered, as in any other colony. There the law officers made a point to openly trade on their position, and not only exacted what the law allowed, but enough beside to increase their own wealth very sensibly.

It chanced that right at this juncture of circumstances, and while Boone was making up his mind what direction he should take in his next move, a hunter, named John Finley, returned from an excursion to the far westward, bringing back the wild and romantic stories of the country that fired more hearts and imaginations than those merely of Daniel Boone. These things always occur just as they are intended to occur, and therefore produce their proper effect. Finley's story failed not of its influence over the mind of Boone. It appears that the former was one of a party of hunters that had roamed away as far as the banks of the Kentucky River, in quest of game. They met with parties of Indians in their wide rambles; but the latter consented to let them pass undisturbed, little thinking of the conflicts that were yet to rage between the two races, or of the vast power that still slumbered, undeveloped, in the breast of the white man. The savages thought this little party not of consequence enough to interfere with, but contented themselves with wondering at their appearance, and silently pitying their numerical weakness. So this handful of hunters made their way undisturbed through a part of the present State of Tennessee, noting the strange country that unrolled its vastness to their vision, and made dumb with astonishment at the grandeur of the forests, the plains, and the rivers. Game was to be had in profuse abundance, and of the best sorts. There was unbounded freedom for their feet on every side. Here they might roam for the rest of their lives, and suffer no interruption from the selfish white man. It was the first party of adventurers who had ever crossed the barriers of the Cumberland range, and explored the richness of the virgin lands of Kentucky. Nothing like tangible results grew out of it; yet its direct influence on the mind of Daniel Boone showed that it was by no means trifling or valueless.

There had been a party of explorers in that distant country (so rumor said), as long as twenty years before, a Dr. Walker having headed a party that traversed the northeastern portion of Kentucky; but nothing came of the undertaking, and, indeed, it cannot be stated with distinctness even on what year the expedition was made. Of the party under Finley, however, Gov. Morehead, of Kentucky, observed in a public address, "That they passed over the Cumberland, and through the intermediate country to the Kentucky River, and penetrated the beautiful Valley of the Elkhorn, there are no sufficient reasons to doubt. It is enough, however, to embalm their memory in our breasts, and to connect their names with the imperishable memorials of our early history, that they were the first adventurers that plunged into the dark and enchanted wilderness of Kentucky; that of all their cotemporaries, they saw her first; and saw her in the pride of her virgin beauty, at the dawn of summer, in the fullness of her vegetation, her soil instinct with fertility, covered with the most luxuriant verdure, the air perfumed with the fragrance of flowers, and her tall forests looming in all their primeval magnificence. How long Finley lived, or where he died, the silence of history does not enable us to know. That his remains are now mingled with the soil that he discovered, there is some reason to hope, for he conducted Boone to Kentucky in 1769, and there the curtain drops upon him forever."

We said that Finley's accounts of the new land to whose grand secrets he had penetrated, fired the imagination and fixed the purpose of Boone. The stories he and his party brought back with them were passed around from one cabin to another, and became the common property of the frontier settlements. The population, already oppressed by the government of the mother country, longed to see the land where tax gatherers and officers of the crown could not come to find them. Many of them thought it would be perfect freedom to be out of the reach of the grasp of any human law whatever, believing there was better justice and more security in a state of nature. They desired to roam without obstruction wherever they might feel inclined. They were men

with big hearts and large powers of imagination in
those days, and they warmed at the thought of perfect freedom for their feet in the wilderness. Among
those who caught these tales of forest life and license
to roam everywhere, none took them more to heart
than did Boone. It appears that in 1764 he had
entered within the present limits of Kentucky, having been sent on a tour of inspection to a branch of
the Cumberland River by a company of land speculators, and at that time he had made the best possible use of his opportunities. The speculation
amounted to nothing, but the man was thus getting
his training for the work he was to do in the future.
He had a taste of the delights of independent exploration, and it only whetted his appetite for more;
and at the right moment came the stories of Finley
and his party of adventurers, exciting his mind to
just that pitch which would be likely to result in
decisive action.

It was months, however, before these tales of the
explorers produced their proper effect. A new party
was a long time in forming. One cause delayed
one, and another cause another. Some disliked to
leave the homes they had already risked so much to
secure; some trusted there would be a change in the
administration of justice at some not distant day, and

thus the prime motive for a change of location would be wanting; all knew something of the perils from the savages that environed them on every side, and with good reason believed that the news of the approach of Finley's party would spread from one tribe to another with amazing rapidity; a second visit, therefore, might not be as happy and peaceful in its consequences as was the first. The affair of another company of explorers was talked of, however, without interruption, and all the points likely to influence the formation and purposes of such a company were discussed with thoroughness.

At last the men were found. There were only six of them all told — six men who thus carried the fortunes of a continent in their hearts! Their names deserve to be remembered of the latest generations. They were — Daniel Boone, John Finley, John Stewart, Joseph Holden, James Monay, and William Cool. The reader will see that Boone's name headed the list, showing the perfect confidence the rest felt in his courage and judgment. It is said he was the last, after all, to come into the plan! It shows that, with all his courage, he did nothing rashly.

When this resolution was formed, Boone had quite a little family around him. His sons were growing

up, and had become old enough now to be of much
assistance to their father. His wife entered sympathetically into the projects of her husband. She
aided him in putting his plans on foot. A true wife
possesses more power to help her husband's aims and
course in life than she herself knows. She agreed
that, as long as it was his wish, he should push out
into the wilderness, and her womanly heart was
ready to sustain him in his resolution. So the
party got ready to start.

There was one John Filson, who attempted to
write the history of this expedition of Boone and his
party, and represented that he took down Boone's
own words; but his style is so inflated and grandiloquent, that it can be read with no pleasure. The
title of the book was: "The Adventures of Col.
Daniel Boone, formerly a Hunter, containing a Narrative of the Wars of Kentucky." It was said to
have deen dictated by Boone himself, and taken down
by Filson from his lips. The story opens in this
way:—

"It was on the first day of May, in the year 1769,
that I resigned my domestic happiness for a time,
and left my family and peaceable habitation on the
Yadkin River, in North Carolina, to wander through
the wilderness of America, in quest of the country

of Kentucky, in company with John Finley, John Stewart, Joseph Holden, James Monay, and William Cool. We proceeded successfully; and after a long and fatiguing journey through a mountainous wilderness, in a westward direction, on the seventh day of June following we found ourselves on Red River, where John Finley had formerly been trading with the Indians, and, from the top of an eminence, saw with pleasure the beautiful level of the Kentucky. Here let me observe that for some time we had experienced the most uncomfortable weather, as a prelibation of our future sufferings. At this place we encamped, made a shelter to defend us from the inclement season, and began to hunt and reconnoitre the country. We found everywhere abundance of beasts of all sorts, through this vast forest. The buffalo were more frequent than I have seen cattle in the settlements, browsing on the leaves of the cane, or cropping the herbage on those extensive plains, fearless, because ignorant of the violence of man. Sometimes we saw hundreds in a drove; and the numbers about the salt springs were amazing. In this forest — the habitation of beasts of every kind natural to America — we practised hunting with great success until the 22d day of September following. This day, John Stewart and I had a pleasing ramble; but fortune changed the scene in the close of it. We had passed through a great forest, on which stood myriads of trees, some gay with blossoms, others rich with fruits. Nature was here a series of wonders, and a fund of delight. Here she displayed her ingenuity and industry in a variety of flowers and fruits, beautifully colored, elegantly shaped, and charmingly flavored; and we were diverted with innumerable animals presenting themselves perpetually to our view. In the decline of the day, near Kentucky River, as we ascended the brow of a small hill, a number of Indians rushed out of a thick cane-brake upon us, and made us prisoners. The time of our sorrow was now arrived, and the scene fully opened. The Indians plundered us of what we had, and kept us in confinement seven days, treating us with common savage usage.

"During this time we discovered (betrayed) no uneasiness or desire to escape, which made them less suspicious of us; but in the dead of night, as we lay in a thick cane-brake by a large fire, when sleep had locked up their senses, my situation not disposing me for rest, I touched my companion and gently awoke him. We improved this favorable opportunity and departed, leaving them to take their rest, and speedily directed our course towards our old camp, but found it plundered, and the company dispersed and gone home. About this time my brother, Squire Boone, with another adventurer, who came to explore the country shortly after us, was wandering through the forest, determined to find me if possible, and accidently found our camp. Notwithstanding the unfortunate circumstances of our company, and our dangerous situation as surrounded with hostile savages, our meeting so fortunately in the wilderness made us reciprocally sensible of the utmost satisfaction." [This is not the simple language of a man like Boone, but rather that of an ambitious biographer, with a style of expression quite as tomid as his ambition.] " Soon after this, my companion in captivity, John Stewart, was killed by the savages, and the man that came with my brother returned home by himself. We were then in a dangerous, helpless situation, exposed daily to perils and death amongst the savages and wild beasts — not a white man in the country but ourselves! Thus situated, many hundred miles from our families, in the howling wilderness, I believe few would have equally enjoyed the happiness we experienced. We continued not in a state of indolence, but hunted every day, and prepared a little cottage to defend us from the winter storms. We remained there undisturbed during the winter.

"On the first day of May, 1770, my brother returned home to the settlement by himself for a new recruit of horses and ammunition, leaving me by myself, without bread, salt or sugar, without company of my fellow creatures, or even horse or dog."

Here is a long story, told in a few words. The details of this weary winter's life, are just what every reader is eager to get hold of. The several points of these severe experiences of many months deserve to be dwelt on with a great deal more minuteness than either Boone or his biographer has seen fit to bestow upon them. The imagination of the reader is left, in a great degree, to fill out the picture; but almost any active imagination can make it a complete one.

The picture of these half dozen hunters, when, according to Boone's account, they found themselves at the place on Red River where Finley had formerly traded with the Indians, and from which eminence they all beheld with delight " the beautiful level of Kentucky," is a rare one in history, and well deserves a place on the artist's canvass. These bold men had been toiling through the forest, and up the mountain side, nearly the whole day, and were weary with their explorations. It was just at sunset when they reached the summit of the mountain. As they all came up to the point from which they stretched out their gaze over the western landscape, a scene met their eyes far surpassing the ideal of the most romantic dreamer. There lay the beautiful Kentucky River, fed by its many branches. There were broad plains, and green slopes, and shaded dells, on which the eye rested with secret satisfaction and delight. Beyond the rolling country close at hand, stretched away a boundless tract of prairie, clothed with luxuriant verdure, where roamed countless herds of buffalo and deer without fear of molestation. The setting sun shed a strange splendor on this wild scene in nature; and the six men thought, as they thus gazed speechless upon its wild beauties, that they had never before experienced so deep and fresh a pleasure. For this very view they had traversed hundreds of miles of trackless wilderness; and when at length their eyes rested upon it, as it lay sleeping in the western sun, they truly felt as if the Canaan of all their hopes had been reached.

On this very spot whence they had caught their first view of beautiful Kentucky, they erected a rude log hut, protecting themselves from the summer rains with strips of bark and intertwisted boughs of the trees. Day after day they sallied forth on hunting excursions, returning in safety again at night, and thus keeping the little party of half a dozen whole and unbroken. They killed deer; they shot buffalo; they trapped and fished; and, in short, they practised all those many arts which belong to the life and secure the subsistence of the pioneer and hunter. They dreaded no dangers as yet; they had seen no Indians, of whom so many stories had been borne to the settlements, and concluded they were not to suffer from molestation at all.

Thus, for a long time, matters went on swimmingly. They were becoming more and more accustomed to their new life, and even began to calculate upon the propriety of returning to North Carolina for their families. Fearing nothing from the approach of the red man, they presently forgot to take those precautions which were, in fact, essential to their daily safety, and so invited dangers when they might just as well repelled them. It was a fatal mistake for this little party of pioneers to separate; yet they were thoughtless enough to do so, and the most disastrous consequences followed. They divided up — one party being composed of Stewart and Boone; the other four men went exploring in another direction. Henceforth their ways diverged forever. Neither party saw the other again.

As Boone has himself narrated, the Indians surprised him and his companion when they ought to have been on the watch, and carried them off prisoners. This was an entirely new phase of life for our forest hero. A man who, all his life, has had the free range of forest and field, would not be likely to keep quiet in a state of sudden imprisonment. His spirit would chafe sorely, and he would find himself impatient once more to be free. But Daniel Boone was a philosopher, and could see at a glance what was most prudent and safe. As soon as he comprehended his novel and dangerous situation, he made up his mind to keep calm and resign himself to his fate. By this means he would disarm the suspicions of the savages, and have more abundant opportunities to make his escape. Patience is a rare virtue, all the books and moralists tell us; and few men would have had the sagacity, as Boone had, to see that his fate hung entirely on his practise of that one quality.

He was a captive for seven days. At the end of that time, they lay down at night in the midst of their tawny guard, and disposed themselves for sleep. At the still midnight hour, when the silence of the wilderness is indeed awful, Boone raised his head and looked around him. By the deep and steady breathing of his savage captors, he knew they were fast locked in slumber. Then, he felt, his opportunity had come. Cautiously awakening his companion, they both regained their feet, took their rifles from the keeping of the Indians, and crept out of the little camp. They both felt that discovery would have been certain death; and therefore they pushed forward in the midnight gloom with redoubled courage and energy. But they succeeded in eluding their captors, and commenced their wanderings together again.

They went to their old camp; but their former companions were gone. Everything betokened disappointment and desolation. The camp had been broken up, and appearances indicated violence and plunder. From this point they never found traces of those four men more. Their fate remains to this day a sealed mystery. Whether they fell victims to the bloody rage of the Indian, who had surprised them in their fancied security, or they had wandered away in different directions, and, weary and despairing, had laid their bones in the undiscovered solitudes of the wilderness, no man lives that can tell. And thus sadly ended the career of the discoverer and early eulogist of Kentucky, John Finley; that man whose vivid reports of this new western paradise kindled enthusiasm in so many bosoms on the banks of the peaceful Yadkin.

Boone and Stewart were therefore left alone. Their sole reliance, both for subsistence and defence, was on their unerring rifles. They built a hut to protect themselves against the influence of the wintry weather, and hunted and watched, waiting patiently for the spring to open. In the month of January, they espied a couple of men coming towards them. Looking closer, they saw they were white men. What must have been the feelings of our hero, to find that one of them was Squire Boone, his youngest brother! Squire brought news from Daniel's wife and children; and Stewart was rejoiced to get intelligence from the settlement. The circumstances that led to the discovery of Boone's little camp by the new comers, were never described; but it seems, at least, like the most marvellous piece of good fortune on record. Yet it was all thus designed, for grand ulterior purposes; it could not by any fatality have been otherwise.

A second time this little party separated. Daniel

Boone and Stewart pursued one course, and Squire Boone and his friend — whose name even is not known — followed another. One would think they had already learned a better lesson. The consequence was, Stewart was surprised and slaughtered by the Indians, while Daniel Boone made his escape; and his brother Squire's companion becoming alarmed, probably thought, in a fit of desperation, to find his way back alone to Carolina, and was never heard of again alive. It is said that a skeleton was long afterwards found in the region, which was believed to have told the tale of his dark and mysterious fate. Thus were the brothers Boone left the only white occupants of that vast territory, the real pioneers in the march of civilization that has been going forward to the West, from that trying and doubtful day to these jubilant and prosperous days of our own.

CHAPTER IV.

ALL ALONE.

SPRING came down upon the forest and the plains again, like a countless flock of birds with bright emerald plumage. The earth laughed once more at her own surpassing beauty. The weary winter had worn away at last, and the spirits of the two men rose with the heightened influences of the new season. They had talked over the needs of the expedition while housed in their cabin through the winter, and at the approach of spring felt prepared for action. In order to effect a real settlement in that region, it was necessary to bring forward recruits, animals and provisions. The question was, how was this best to be done? During their winter discussions at their fire, they had canvassed it very freely, and concluded at last what was best to be attempted.

The powder was low, and bullets were scarce for the rifles; if these two items failed, all was lost. Hence it was important that something should be done as soon as possible. Daniel Boone was all ready for the sacrifice, and his brother Squire was quite as willing to perform his part. The plan was matured. Daniel would remain where he was, and Squire would travel back alone to North Carolina, to obtain recruits and supplies. It was a distance of many hundred miles. A bolder project was never undertaken than that which makes the names of these two devoted Boone brothers immortal.

So the younger one started off on his solitary tramp homeward, taking the blessing of his brother to the wife and children at home; while the other remained behind, to eke out long days, and weeks, and months in utter solitude, hopeful and patient for the turn of affairs that was to come. Both were heroic in their resolutions; it would be hard to say whose lot was the harder, or which one took upon himself the greater dangers. It was something to begin a solitary march through a pathless wilderness, five hundred miles homeward, exposed to all sorts of obstacles and dangers, dependent on the rifle alone for food, and trusting to Providence for shelter alike from wild beasts and the elements. It was no less an undertaking to resolve to sit down calmly and patiently where he was, with no companion even in the form of a dog, no voice to respond to one's own, no human face in which to read sympathetic answers to the emotions of one's own soul, and to live on in this way for slowly revolving weeks, and months, doubtful whether the brave messenger homewards would ever reach his destination.

We could wish to read nothing more vivid, if it could be had, than the record of the secret experiences of our hero, during this protracted period of solitude. All stories of fights, of battles, of sieges, and of storms, would pale before the living realities of this one man's inward struggles and contests. To-day, all hope and buoyancy, with the smiles of nature finding their way into his receptive heart; to-morrow, cast down with the weight of a sadder mood, left to wonder if dark fate had finally overtaken him, and almost ready to give over all as lost. Few men have lived to feel what Boone felt in the period of his solitary stay in the wilderness of Kentucky. He best expresses it himself in the few and simple words taken down by Filson, — "Alone by myself, without bread, salt, or sugar, without company of any fellow creatures, or even a horse or dog." That was solitude indeed. If any one should feel inclined to doubt its reality, let him go out of our cities into a common woodland, and try it even there for a single day. Besides all this, it was well known to our hero that if he should be captured by the Indians again, there was no chance for him; having once given them the slip successfully, he could not hope to accomplish the like feat again. One comrade, Stewart, had already been butchered before his eyes, and the fate of the other four was involved in a mystery hardly less painful. Of course he could not fail to keep all this fixed steadily before his thought, and to measure his own chances by the same standard. But we will let him describe his sensations for himself, as set down by his biographer, Filson:

"I confess I never before was under greater necessity of exercising philosophy and fortitude. A few days I passed uncomfortably. The idea of a beloved wife and family, and their anxiety upon the account of my absence and exposed situation, made sensible impressions on my heart. A thousand dreadful apprehensions presented themselves to my view, and had undoubtedly disposed me to melancholy, if farther indulged. One day I undertook a tour through the country, and the diversity and beauties of nature I met with in this charming season expelled every gloomy and vexatious thought. Just at the close of day the gentle gales retired, and left the place to the disposal of a profound calm. Not a breeze shook the most tremulous leaf. I had gained the summit of a commanding ridge, and, looking round with astonishing delight, beheld the ample plains, the beauteous tracts below. On the other hand, I surveyed the famous river Ohio, that rolled in silent dignity, marking the western boundary of Kentucky with inconceivable grandeur. At a vast distance I beheld the mountains lift their venerable brows, and penetrate the clouds. All things were still. I kindled a fire near a fountain of sweet water, and feasted on the loin of a buck which a few hours before I had killed. The sullen shades of night soon overspread the whole hemisphere, and the earth seemed to gasp after the hovering moisture.

"My roving excursion this day had fatigued my body and diverted my imagination. I laid me down to sleep, and awoke not until the sun had chased away the night. I continued this tour, and in a few days explored a considerable part of the country, each day equally pleased as the first. I returned to my old camp, which was not disturbed in my absence. I did not confine my lodging to it, but often reposed in thick cane-brakes, to avoid the savages, who, I believe, often visited my camp, but, fortunately for me, in my absence. In this situation I was constantly exposed to danger and death."

There seems to be some fatality about unpractised persons trying to use the pen. A man of

Boone's perfect simplicity of character could have told his story to a group of listeners without any trouble whatever; but the moment he attempts to put his woodland experiences on paper, even though it be by the hand of another, he parts with his simplicity and straightway becomes turgid and, in a degree, bombastic. The fault may be chiefly Filson's, who wrote down his narrative; for it is not to be supposed, knowing what we do of his slender education, that Boone could tell what was the best style to write his story, and, like most others of his class, he thought, of course, that the most inflated and sounding must produce the greatest effect. It is reasonable to conclude that Boone merely gave his biographer the outline of his forest life, and that the latter expanded, and colored, and over-dressed it to suit his own tawdry taste.

From Boone's account, therefore, we know that he did not stay long in one place, during the absence of his brother. He traversed the eastern portion of the State, and obtained a view of the great Ohio River. Three months he wandered about in these vast solitudes, shut out from the sight of a single human face in all that time. If ever a man was in the truest and strictest sense a pioneer, that man was Daniel Boone.

Young Squire Boone came back. He had traversed that long distance, to and fro, without a companion, and at last he stood by his brother's side again. He had faithfully kept his promise to return. He brought along with him a pair of horses, with provisions. He brought welcome news from the brave hunter's wife and family. He brought tidings of the murmur of the people at the foreign rule that oppressed them, and possibly of the recent Boston Massacre, which sent a thrill of horror through the country. The horses were invaluable, and yet a source of the greatest anxiety; for they were just what would be most likely to betray them into the hands of the Indians. They could not be hidden, as the brothers could hide themselves. They would not fail to testify their presence at any and at all times to the Indian. For eight months these two men roamed over the tract of territory upon which they had entered, and were not once molested. It is the strangest of all facts recorded in the history of settlements, and goes to show that Boone had, in reality, hit upon his true destiny as a pioneer.

Having traversed the country lying between the Green and Cumberland rivers, and found those curious peculiarities of a limestone soil, known in Kentucky by the name of *sink-holes*, the brothers came back to the Kentucky River again, where they determined to establish themselves permanently. This, to their eyes, was the most attractive of all the spots they had yet seen. Here they remained until they had become pretty familiar with the country; they were attached to the new land, and had waited to behold the beauty of its promises, and were satisfied. This was in the year 1771.

Finally, Daniel Boone began to think of the old home he had left in North Carolina. The recollection of his wife and children tugged steadily at his heart; he felt an inclination to return, which he could no longer resist. Not that he had any desire to remain in Carolina, for such was not the fact; it was already his determination to bring back the loved ones with him, and, with them, to take quiet and permanent possession of the beautiful country he had discovered. He returned. His old friends received him with the delight and wonder with which they would have one, of whom they had given up all hopes. He had many an exciting adventure to relate to them about his life in the wilderness; and the stories of the dangers he had passed through, while they filled all listeners with fear, were nevertheless calculated to inflame their imaginations.

Boone hoped, no doubt, to have succeeded in making up a little party of settlers without a great deal of delay or difficulty; but in this respect he did not realize all his hopes. Of course, the wife and children were ready to return with him, even though they went without the presence of a single other family to cheer them. But that was not enough for him. He had tried the perils of the wilderness of Kentucky for himself, and knew that in numbers and courage alone there was safety; hence it was his wish to enlist as many families as he could in the project of forming a new settlement. To effect this, he had first to persuade all the dwellers along the course of the peaceful Yadkin that the plan was, under proper circumstances, a prudent as well as profitable one. This he found to be slow and difficult work, indeed. They received his glowing accounts of the country with an exciting pleasure, but still could not bring themselves to believe that it was altogether safe to go out as yet and possess it.

For the long term of two years, therefore, did he patiently remain at home, before he was able to prevail on them to make a start. Other men would have given it up in despair, but he knew better how to advance a purpose in which his soul was so bound up. He was willing to wait, because he knew the object aimed at was worth the pains. And although it lay not in his power to overcome the fears of the Yadkin settlers, when the fate of Stewart and Finley was talked about, he still felt sure that time would aid him in the work he had set before him to do, and therefore remained quiet among them, ever ready to answer all their questions respecting Kentucky, yet waiting and hoping for the change in public sentiment to work itself out. For two years, as we said, he thus patiently waited; a long time to some, but not long when compared with the greatness of the plans that were thus to be accomplished.

At length the little party was made up. It consisted of only the two Boone families — those of Daniel and Squire; those who had thought they would go, not feeling quite ready when the time really came. The Boones, however, determined to set the example, and to leave that, and their description of the new country westward, to do their own work upon the minds of the people in the Yadkin settlements. They set forth on the 25th day of September, 1773, taking along with them some cattle and horses.

Courage generally makes its own conquests; and by the time this little party reached Powell's Valley, they found, to their astonishment and delight, that the stories of the new country had persuaded five more families to join the projected expedition, together with a band of some forty strong and determined men, all well armed for the enterprise and its dangers. It was truly a great accession. At the head of this band of pioneers Daniel Boone was placed, by virtue of his character and experience, and at once led them out into the western wilderness, across the long dreaded mountains. A more interesting sight than the departure of this stouthearted little company of pioneers the world had not witnessed since the departure of the Pilgrims from Delft Haven for the sterile shores of New England. It comprised all the elements necessary to build up a great and powerful nation.

But a cloud rested upon them ere long, whose shadow served to obscure all their plans. They had proceeded safely on their journey till the tenth day of October, seeing nothing of the Indians, so much dreaded by all, when a most sad fatality overtook them, rending the heart of the leader with grief. It seems that a part of the company, seven in number, had gone back a little way to collect together some of the cattle that had wandered a little from the main body; and, fearing no danger because they had hitherto met with none, they became in a degree thoughtless about keeping the usual watch. In an unguarded moment they were set upon by a party of savages, who had stealthily tracked them along, and, without the slightest warning, six out of the seven were cruelly butchered! Of these six, a young son of Daniel Boone, only seventeen years of age, was one. The main body of the pioneers heard the sounds proceeding from the fight while it was going on, and at once rushed to the scene; but they reached the spot only to find that all had been slain but one, and the young and brave son of Boone among them. The seventh had managed to make his escape.

Here was a sorrowful beginning indeed. Slaughter on the very threshold of the undertaking. It is not within the power of writer to describe the anguish of the bereft mother, the speechless grief of the father, who felt that he carried the responsibility of the whole enterprise on his own shoulders, or the terror that struck into the hearts of the entire company. There was grief and fear in that little band, brave and self-reliant as they confessedly were, which none of them were able to overcome. The first question each one seemed to put himself was, what is to be done next? They did not dare to think of going on, for the forest might be swarming with bloodthirsty savages. Boone listened to all, his own heart swelling with sorrow. He could not push forward with blind recklessness; he did not feel like asking others to share unseen dangers which he had found to be so very bitter in tasting himself; and, above all, his heart yearned towards the dear wife at his side, whose boy had just been sacrificed to the ruthlessness of the savages; how could he, therefore, affect a courage which he had not, especially when it could not benefit the rest of the company by infusing a new courage into them?

No; Daniel Boone was but a man, and a true one; there was nothing like braggardism in his nature; he knew better than to set at defiance the deep and thorough instincts of our common nature, and therefore he submitted, and in silence obeyed them. The company turned their faces the other way. Boone would even then have gone forward, had all the the rest been willing; but he showed himself a greater man, and a more capable and courageous pioneer, by finally yielding to the feelings of those who had made him their leader. Yet he never in his heart intended to give his purpose up; he knew the day was not very far off when it must be resumed again.

It was resolved to fall back upon the Clinch River,

in Virginia, where was a settlement of many years' standing. The larger portion of the little band returned to this spot never to go forth into the western wilderness again; but Boone only bided his time. Lord Dunmore was then the Royal Governor of Virginia, just as the other colonies had officers of foreign appointment. It was the avowed policy of the English Government to reward the men who had distinguished themselves on behalf of her arms in the old French War, with gifts of wild land; and Lord Dunmore exercised the authority granted him for this purpose, by making liberal grants to such as he personally knew to have proved their bravery in the English cause. Hence, at the very time when this little party of pioneers returned disheartened from their march, and entered the settlements on Clinch River, there was much doing in the way of locating the lands of which Lord Dunmore was about to put them in possession. Boone reached them at exactly the right time. They had had a present, but did not know what it was worth. Boone was able to tell them all about its value. They were told that lands somewhere in the west were theirs of right, in requital of their services in the war; Boone alone was able to inform them where they were, and how they were to be reached. This was not the first tract of land, by any means, that was bestowed on the brave soldiers of that time.

To locate and measure off the land, however, for the use of the soldiers to whom it was to be given, it was necessary to send out a party of practised surveyors; and this the Governor proceeded to do forthwith. A party was detailed who went into the country now known by the name of Kentucky, headed by Capt. Thomas Bullitt. The party included the names of such men as Harrod, Taylor, Bullitt, and McAffee, — men who afterwards made a memorable mark in the history of Kentucky. They found the stories of Boone, glowing as they were, to be true. They found immense cane-brakes, threaded by well worn tracks of the buffalo, which tracks they called "streets." They came upon salt licks near the streams, where the wild animals were wont to go and obtain that necessary commodity — salt; and witnessed at these places the frequent contests that arose among the brutes for supremacy.

This party went out in the year 1773. During the next year, another followed. Capt. James Harrod, at the head of a body of forty men, came down the Ohio River in the month of May, from the Monongohela, and proceeded to lay out the town then known as Harrodstown, but now as Harrodsburgh. They laid out the place in lots of half an acre each, and allowed for each another outlying lot of five acres; a liberal style of setting a new town on foot, and proving that land was to be had in plenty. It naturally makes men's ideas large to be placed where nothing but the horizon bounds their view on every side. Besides this second party of surveyors under Harrod, there was still a third, that explored along the course of the Kentucky River, starting from where Louisville stands to day. Thus was the new country coming under the experienced eyes of surveyors very rapidly. It was literally staked out among them, and each selected some particular portions for his own. The work was all done in behalf of the men who had served the mother country against the French and Indians; they were waiting to go forth and enter upon their possessions. But it was accompanied with danger. The Indians lurked on every side. The surveying parties felt their savage cruelty, and the little exploring party of Boone had previously yielded up a costly sacrifice to them, as we have already narrated.

In the vicinity of the settlements on Clinch River, Boone remained for more than six months. It was a sore trial to a daring spirit like his to be thus hemmed in, without the power to move, for so long a period. He had expected far different things in this time; his thoughts had led him out into that beautiful land of Kentucky where he was to make his home, and there he had hoped to be with his family at the very time he was thus shut up in the settlements of Virginia; yet he was patient; no man knew better than Boone that nothing so wastes one's power as to chafe at delays, of instead calmly resigning himself to them.

The Government of the Old Dominion had heard of the rare courage and hardihood of Daniel Boone, stories of whose skill and perseverance as a pioneer had been passed around from one little settlement to another; and Governor Dunmore resolved forthwith to send for a man whose character was so firm, and whose services could be turned to so good account. It was an unexpected summons to our hero, who had no reason to suppose himself in any way marked above other men. His friends received the tidings with a great deal of satisfaction, since it showed in what high esteem their brave leader was held by the powers of the State. It could have brought little pleasure, however, to the wife and mother, for her heart was thus made to open its wounds anew. No march into the wilderness now but would bring back to her vision the cruel picture of her murdered boy.

CHAPTER V.

TRANSYLVANIA.

WITH the request of Governor Dunmore Daniel Boone complied immediately. He was already weary with waiting for the waters to move again. A single person, Michael Stoner by name, was associated with him. He afterwards gave his own name to a branch, or fork, of the Licking River, and was well known as a frontiersman. In return for the valiant services he performed as a pioneer, he received a liberal tract of land in Kentucky, lying on Stoner's Fork.

The winter was filled up with plans and projects, which Boone himself felt to be feasible, but which he had no certainty of ever being able to carry out. When Lord Dunmore, however, signified to him that his services were wanted by the Government as a pioneer, he was all ready to go. He knew very well what dangers from the Indians beset the surveying parties already in Kentucky, and the need there was of carrying aid of some sort to them; therefore he did not feel the least inclination to wait for circumstances to change; he was sure the work to be done ought to be done at once. Stoner and he set out together: not a very strong force to support a party in peril from the savages, yet making up in courage and assurance what they lacked in numbers.

The distance from Clinch River to the Falls of the Ohio is about eight hundred miles; such miles as are not travelled in these times across the Western States, crowded with obstacles and dangers, and most difficult to be traversed by reason of every circumstance. Yet these two men overcame the distance in sixty-two days, and arrived at the settlement in safety. It was hardly less enterprising a journey than that made by Boone's younger brother alone, through the wilderness from Kentucky to North Carolina. The path to the West was now opened, and he saw it. The fruits of his own work he beheld on every hand. Harrod was the first one with whom Boone and his companion communicated, and to him he made known the danger that threatened from the hostile Indians on the north. This was, in fact, the main object of his errand. Governor Dunmore had heard of the threats of the savages, and desired that the surveying party should be apprised of them as soon as possible, that every precaution might be taken against their results.

The assaults were made by the savages, just as was

feared. A party belonging to the Harrod company were surprised, in the vicinity of a spring they had recently discovered. One of the men, in his fright, made for the river, and it is reported that he sailed with all possible speed down the Ohio and the Mississippi, and made his way in his open boat by sea around to Philadelphia! But such a story is beyond belief. It was as easy to credit so enormous a narrative, in those days, as to receive one of more modest dimensions.

The northwestern tribes of Indians came down upon the settlers with hearts full of hatred. The principal tribe that opened hostilities was the Shawnees, who dwelt along the banks of the Great and Little Miami rivers; but there were other tribes in the northwest that joined them. These savages had every reason to feel jealous and unquiet. Here were men of a strange race come among them, occupying their lands and crowding them along. Their customs were in all respects dissimilar, and they could hold no sympathies in common. The white man would of course have preferred to dwell alone and in peace, but the red man could not stand by and see an enemy encroaching upon his hunting-grounds, without resisting him. It is a sad tale, that of the fading away of the race of red men, and it never will be told in all its details.

Having done his work so well, Boone received at the hands of Governor Dunmore an appointment to a military command. Three distinct posts, or garrisons, were placed under him; a great responsibility to be put upon any one man, but no more than Boone was fully capable of sustaining. These garrisons were all posted on the frontier, and of course were very much exposed to danger from the Indians. It was not long before a pitched battle was fought. The locality of the fight was at the point where the Great Kenhawa joins with the Ohio River, and it is spoken of in the annals of Virginia as the bloodiest and most hotly-contested battle of any known in her history. The name of the Indian leader in this famous fight was Cornstalk, acknowledged to be at the head of the whole Indian confederacy. Of the whites engaged in this forest encounter, seventy-five were slain outright, and one hundred and forty were wounded. Eleven hundred men took part in the battle, on the side of the whites, led by Gen. Andrew Lewis, one of the bravest of the brave Virginians. They needed their best leader in that time of trial, for the Indians were marshalled by one of their most noted chieftains.

TRANSYLVANIA. 85

This bloody battle was a decisive one, and the savages were, for the time, repulsed and taught their place. As the evidence of winter approached, Boone, having conscientiously discharged the duties on which he was sent out by Lord Dunmore, made ready to return to his friends on Clinch River, where he purposed to pass the winter in quiet. In the peaceful life of the settlements he would find leisure to set on foot new and greater plans for the realization of his dreams. His thoughts would be free to run back over the past, and from those experiences he could draw figures of the untried future. Kentucky was his continual dream. Her plains and prairies lay mapped out in his mind, in all their beauty and magnificence. He knew for himself, from having studied it with his own eyes and measured it with his own feet, that his discovery of that land was to make a vast difference with the future of the white race. He had a prescience of the greatness and power that were yet to come. And the winter would not fail to be profitable to him in the highest sense, while he was thus left to think over his plans without molestation. The activity of the mind of Boone, during that winter, was of just as great account in its results, as if he had been physically engaged all the while in exploration. Scott tells a story of the traveller, Mungo Park, that being caught by a friend idly skipping smooth stones across a certain river, he confessed he was only engaged, in his mind, in trying to solve the problem of the sources of the Nile. These idle hours are often full of the pith and moment of action, and are consequently better than all the others together. The winter thus wore away. It was now well understood that no land had yet been discovered that, for climate and soil, was such a prize for settlers; and the authorities, as well as the people of Virginia, resolved to go forth and take possession of such a noble patrimony. Accordingly, there was much talk made about the new land everywhere. The subject was discussed in all its bearings. All were awake to the enterprise, and freely counted up the advantages that were sure to grow out of an undertaking to settle the country. The authorities, in particular, saw an addition to their own power in the settlement of the new State, and resolved at once to avail themselves of their chances. Accordingly a bounty of four hundred acres of land was offered to every person who would go out and become a settler; that is, to any one who would build a hut, or cabin, clear a sufficient piece of land for the sustenance of a family, and raise a single crop of corn. The right to the land under such conditions, is what was called a "settlement right," and a great many such were made about that particular time.

It is necessary at this point of our narrative, to introduce another character upon the stage, and a man whose influence over the western country was hardly surpassed by the long and unparalleled career of Daniel Boone himself. That man was Richard Henderson. He was a native genius. His natural gifts were sufficiently generous to have placed him in the front rank of any society into which he might have been thrown. He was a full grown man, in fact, before he knew how to read or write; and it became necessary for him to teach himself in these rudimentary branches of learning, at a time in life when most men would have felt the inclination for anything else. Born in North Carolina, he found himself early in life the possessor of the little local office — no doubt very important at that period — of constable. This, at least, served to bring him out into the notice of the people. As opportunities offered, he showed that he was possessed of the gift of eloquence; he could wield a powerful influence over those around him by his personal address, and, knowing what resources were thus placed at his command, he determined to study and enter upon the practice of the law. His talents were truly wonderful, and his manners were of the most engaging and popular character. Everybody was his friend. So rapidly did he rise in his profession, in a short time he was made one of the Judges of the State. This would have been likely to satisfy the ambition of any man of no more than ordinary talent, who would have duly composed his thoughts and considered his worldly purposes all answered; but it was not so with Henderson; he grew restless, was lavish with his money, could not bear the trammels of social life and customs with which he was surrounded, and finally conceived a plan of emigration westward. It was a plan, too, in all respects worthy of the greatness of the man's nature. Ordinary schemes of the same kind grow dim before the brilliancy of the project set on foot by him.

In order, therefore, to retrieve his fortunes and make himself a name worth recording, he resolved to lead out and found a colony. He was, in those times, a bold man who would seriously entertain such a project. Gov. Morehead, of Kentucky, describes the plan thus: "In the autumn of the year 1774, there originated in North Carolina one of the most extraordinary schemes of ambition and speculation which was exhibited in an age pregnant with such events. Eight private gentlemen — Richard Henderson, William Johnstone, Nathaniel Hart, John Tuttrel, David Hart, John Williams, James Hogg, and Leonard Henley Bullock contrived the project of purchasing a large tract of country in the west from the Cherokee Indians, and provisionary arrangements were made, with a view to the accomplishment of their object, for a treaty to be held with them the ensuing year. This was the celebrated Transylvania Company, which formed so singular a connection with our early annals. In March, 1775, Col. Henderson, on behalf of his associates, met the chiefs of the Cherokees, who were attended by twelve hundred warriors, at a fort on the Wataga, the south-eastern branch of the Holston River. A council was held, the terms were discussed, and the purchase was consummated, including the whole tract of country between the Cumberland and Kentucky rivers."

This superb tract of land was, for size, of the dimensions of a kingdom; and it is said that its purchase was secured with a very trifling amount of valuables. Its soil was of the best; the plains and slopes were pictures of beauty; rivers and small streams interlaced on every portion of its surface.

To the enterprising settler of that time, it must have seemed a perfect paradise. It lay on the back of Virginia, North and South Carolina, comprehending the Kentucky, Cherokee, and Ohio rivers, besides smaller streams and rivulets unnumbered, and was about one hundred miles square; a truly royal domain, and worthy of the best blood running in the veins of man. Henderson threw open this magnificent tract to settlement, and proceeded to invite colonists into it from all quarters. Nor was he compelled to wait long in order to secure success. Very soon he became, by right of his character, the Governor of the entire colony. There are various stories about Boone's connection with the origin of this grand plan of colonization, yet nothing on the subject may be said to be definitely known. Some suppose that he was secretly employed by the persons interested in getting up this project, and that they subsequently acted on the information he brought them respecting the value of the lands. If he *was* the agent of such a company, it may be safely asserted that he performed his work faithfully; they could not have found a man more capable or reliable.

The next thing was, after obtaining possession of the lands, to settle them. To do this, it was necessary that some well-known leader should be found, who had the ability and fearlessness to pioneer for the colonists, showing them the value of the new territory and the perfect safety in going out to take possession of it. Very naturally, the thoughts of the leaders in this great enterprise centered upon Daniel Boone. His fame had already gone abroad. What any one man was thought able to do, in threading the wilderness, it was readily believed Boone could do of all others. Besides, he knew this country from actual observation. He had lived in it, long months at a time, with not the sound of a white man's voice to cheer his heart. He had hunted the wild game in its dense coverts and mighty fastness. The streams ran before his own eyes, and he had let his secret thoughts and dreams sail grandly down their peaceful currents. Knowing this, it was most natural that they should apply to him for the aid he alone could render them.

Accordingly, he signified his willingness to start off on the errand confided to him. Again he must exile himself from his family, and run the gauntlet of those terrible dangers of whose presence in the wilderness his wife already knew. He loved his wife and children as much as any man; yet it was contrary to his nature to remain idly at home, when there were great things for him to aid in doing abroad. He therefore took leave of them, prepared to risk his fortunes once more in the land of the savages. A party of men, all provided with arms and ammunition, was made up for him, which he was asked to command. Their first object was to open a road between the Cumberland Ridge and Kentucky; a road that could be travelled by those adventurous settlers who were eager to follow the path thus made.

It was no light work, in the first place, to surmount the mountains. A natural gap, or passageway, had before been discovered, and it was in its vicinity that Boone's little party of pioneers were surprised before by the Indians, and compelled to return to Clinch River, with the loss of six out of seven young men of the company. There were perils enough on the hither side of this undertaking; they would be many times multiplied when they came to the other. The wildness of the mountain scenery, however, was a source of inspiration to a soul like that of Boone. In the frowning shadows, made more terrible still to the uncultivated imagination by the cry of wolves and the shriek of owls, he found recesses where his courageous heart could feel itself enjoying only the unmolested solitude he craved. The forest, however lonely to other men, had no terrors for him. Even the presence of Indians failed to inspire him with the fear and timidity from which all the rest were wont to suffer. They passed on through the gorge in the mountain-chain, its solitudes echoing almost sepulchrally to the sound of their voices. The woods loomed solemnly and grand above their heads. Precipices yawned hungrily below them. Chasms, with deep and dark pools in their hearts, slept sullenly at their feet. The morning sun visited the ravines late, when all the rest of nature was alive and exulting in the glory of its light. And still this little file of resolute men kept steadily on, led by the single ray that ever beams out of a fixed purpose. Into the gloomy solitudes they plunged without hesitation, scarce heeding or dreaming that a great nation was to be drawn magnetically after them. There have been pioneer parties since that day, but few whose track westward has been followed with more lively interest than this.

The world could not travel without roads; in fact, the road is the first signal of civilization. Boone and his men, therefore, opened their path as they went along. They became surveyors, at the same time that they were hunters with the rifle. Slowly they advanced, and patiently they kept at their work. The man who should have presumed to go in quest of them, starting from the settlements in Virginia, would have been able easily to track them all the way along. They saw the work of their hands, and felt a glow of pride and satisfaction at what they had accomplished. The sunlight was let in upon the forest in a narrow strip, following which would conduct any traveller safely along to the new settlement about to be established by the Transylvania Company in Kentucky.

They experienced no difficulty whatever from the opposition of the Indians, until they had advanced to a point within fifteen miles of Boonesborough; here they were most unexpectedly assailed by them, and put to the necessity of making an earnest and vigorous defence. The red men knew not what this mysterious road meant. It awakened the deepest suspicions. Hence they concluded it was best to end it where it was, by putting its makers out of existence. While the party of surveyors were off their guard, engaged with the main business for which they had travelled so far, the Indians made a sudden dash at them from the thicket, and, after a close and bloody struggle, succeeded in killing two of their number before they could be repulsed. Boone, however, did not yield his ground. To hold that, he felt to be of the first importance. He likewise knew that he should be attacked by the Indians a second time, if he did not attack them; and on the third day following he ventured an assault, whereby he lost a couple of men more, making four in all — a loss such as no company of the size of that one could well bear. He describes the two battles in a letter to Col. Henderson, as follows: —

"APRIL 1ST, 1775.

"DEAR COLONEL,—After my compliments to you, I shall acquaint you with my misfortunes. On March the 25th, a party of Indians fired on my company about half an hour before day, and killed Mr. Twitty and his negro, and wounded Mr. Walker very deeply, but I hope he will recover.

"On March the 28th, as we were hunting for provisions, we found Samuel Tale's son, who gave us an account that the Indians had fired on their camp on the 27th day. My brother and I went down and found two men killed and scalped — Thomas McDowell and Jeremiah McPeters. I have sent a man down to all the lower companies, in order to gather them all to the mouth of the Otter Creek. My advice to you, sir, is to come, or send, as soon as possible. Your company is desired greatly, for the people are very uneasy, but are willing to stay and venture their lives with you; and now is the time to flustrate their (the Indians') intentions, and keep the country whilst we are in it. If we give way to them now, it will ever be the case. This day we start from the battle-ground for the mouth of the Otter Creek, where we shall immediately erect a fort which will be done before you can come, or send; then we can send ten men to meet you, if you send for them.

"I am, sir, your most obedient,
"DANIEL BOONE.

"N. B. We stood on the ground and guarded our baggage till day, and lost nothing. We have about fifteen miles to Cantrick's, at Otter Creek."

The modesty of the writer is to be particularly noticed; he is at no pains to bring himself forward, if indeed he once thought about himself, or his deeds, at all. On the same day on which the above letter was written, the fort alluded to was commenced. The party sprang to the work with earnest vigor, feeling how important its completion was to their own safety. The structure was built close by the river, one end resting on the bank, and the whole extending back for a distance of two hundred and sixty feet. It was a hundred and fifty feet wide. The style of it is as follows; large pieces of timber were sharpened and one end driven into the ground, very much like common pickets, and within the enclosure thus formed were the several cabins and huts of the party. It may not seem as if such a defence could amount to a great deal, but it did, for all that; the Indians knew nothing of the hiding places that might be stowed away in this rude fort, while, at the same time, it afforded the settler a better advantage over his artful enemy; the forest and the cane-brake were well understood by the savage, who there had everything on his side: but the fort was a puzzle whose key he did not know how to get hold of. Still, there was one strong objection to this fort: it was close by the woods at one end, thus affording the savage every chance to approach the settlers, and still be concealed from them.

At each corner of this great enclosure was built a strong log hut, with its hewn ends projecting outwardly, thus making the whole a more enduring defence than before. The cabins, or huts, were likewise constructed side by side, with rough and heavy logs, making it next to impossible to overcome their united strength. Then the few gates needed were stout and heavy, difficult to be moved at all, and capable of successfully resisting any assault, even from overwhelming numbers. To build this fort required from the 1st of April till the 14th of June. In other words, it was begun just before the battle of Lexington, and completed just before the battle of Bunker Hill. Important events were transpiring, at that time, as well on the seaboard as far back in the wilderness. One man lost his life at the hands of the Indians, while the work was going on, and that was all. The natives of the forest could not but regard the building of this fort among them, in the very heart of their noble hunting-grounds, with greater jealousy even than the laying out of the road; hence they were aroused to making concerted movements to destroy it and its white inmates together. To have lost but one man by them, during the progress of the work, therefore, was a great deal less misfortune than might reasonably have been expected.

Thus, then, were the projectors of Transylvania put in possession of their territory. A fort had been built in that remote wilderness, properly garrisoned, and successfully held against the assaults of the Indians. Boone, by this time, felt as if he would like to go back and see his wife and children again. To this end, he determined to leave the garrison where they were, duly cautioning them against surprises at the hands of the savages, and impressing on them the necessity of having a certain amount of cleared land close by.

We have not the particulars of this journey of Boone back to Virginia; it is enough to know that it was made in safety, and that his heart was gladdened once more to find himself in the arms of his beloved wife and children. He resolved, this time, to be separated from them no more. He meant, when he returned, to take them along with him. It shows a truly delicate trait of character in Boone, to wait until all due preparations had been made for his wife and children in the wilderness before he came to carry them out with him, and makes him appear to be anything but the rude and rough person usually looked for in a pioneer. There was a delicacy about his noble nature that would well have become a woman. He had never asked his wife to accompany him, until he had first made all proper provision for her comfort and safety. Now that the new fort at Boonesborough was completed, and defended by an armed and watchful garrison, he felt secure in the thought of taking his little brood out into the forest wilds, and knew, too, what a blessed influence the presence of wife and children would have over him. The path westward was now open; men and women could go forward in it and people the country.

Boone's wife and daughters were all ready to start. How that journey was made, we have, unfortunately, no particular record. Boone himself says of it, in his narrative, only this,—that it was "safe, and without any other difficulties than such as are common to the passage." They stood, at length, on the banks of the Kentucky River. No white females had put their feet there before them. Of the women of this country, they were the pioneers; a young wife, and daughters in the very blush of girlhood and innocence. How rough and hard their woodland life was, it is not easy at this day to imagine. It was an unusual thing for any one then to be taken sick and die in his own bed; when death overtook men in the forest, it was always a death of violence. In illustration of the feelings begotten of such a state of things, the following impressive incident is related:

"An old lady, who had been in the forts, was, not many years ago, describing the scenes she had witnessed in those times of peril and adventure; and, among other things, remarked that, during the first two years of her residence in Kentucky, the most comely sight she beheld was seeing *a young man dying in his bed a natural death.* She had been familiar with blood, and carnage, and death, but in all these cases the sufferers were the victims of the Indian tomahawk and scalping-knife; and that on an occasion when a young man was taken sick and died after the usual manner of nature, she and the rest of the women sat up all night, gazing upon him *as an object of beauty!*"

That must indeed have been a rugged way of life which subjected women to trials like these; which made it desirable even to see a person die in a bed, because death by the tomahawk and the scalping-knife had become so common.

Boone brought out with him, on this return journey to the fort, several of the families that turned back before, when the little party was assailed by the Indians. These families knew him well, had seen him tried in the fiery furnace of affliction, and were content to repose their safety in his keeping. But they had not all gone very far together, before they separated. The precise reason for this step is not known, and probably never will be. Boone pushed on, while the remainder, or the greater part of them, lagged behind. They lost their way. Their cattle and stock strayed away from them.

They were like sheep without a shepherd. And after many reverses, sufferings, and irritating disappointments, they managed at last to reach the fort at Boonesborough by the pathway that was marked out for them. They had at least learned one lesson by this idle dissatisfaction; they knew the worth of the man they had deserted.

One fort naturally suggested another. Each was the nucleus, or center, for a wide settlement. This position of Boone being so strong, it lent encouragement to the rest to believe they might establish others equally strong. So they began to radiate. Pretty soon, there was a fort here, and another fort there; yet the increase was steady and slow, for each new post was, at best, but a rash experiment. It was not so plain, even yet, that the settlements did not exist as much by the leniency of the Indians, as by the aid of anything else. Were they disposed, there was little doubt that they might at any time have overwhelmed the little band of white men with their numbers.

Other men soon began to come into the fort now; such men as Callaway, and Henderson himself. As soon as the latter arrived, it was apparent that Transylvania was a settlement in good earnest, and not a mere project in the brain or on paper. From this time, work seemed to begin. The first thing was, to make the land produce something; therefore they set about clearing away the forest in the vicinity of the fort, and ploughing it up for planting corn. The work now looked like the work performed by the settlers of Jamestown, under Capt. John Smith. All was activity and bustle. There was hunting in the woods, and the settlers were of course chiefly sustained for a time by game; but it would not be long before their wants would be answered from the soil. Sometimes the hunters carelessly wandered away from the fort, forgetful that the Indian watched when they were unguarded. Boone continued to caution them respecting this practise, and it is safe to assert that many a time they owed their lives to his supervising care and watchfulness.

CHAPTER VI.

TROUBLE WITH THE INDIANS.

GREAT deeds were done, during this same year, in the Atlantic Colonies. The two great battles of the Revolution had been fought — that of Lexington, and that of Bunker Hill — each of which was like a magnet, to draw to a focus the patriotic sentiments and fraternal feelings of the people of all the colonies. The settlers in far-off Kentucky heard the glorious news, and it warmed their hearts. Lexington had a voice for them like that of a trumpet, stirring their blood. In fact, one small party of hunters, who had camped down not far from the head-waters of the Elkhorn, testified their ardor and sympathy by naming the little settlement after the first battle-field for liberty, and by the name of Lexington it goes to this day.

Then came still worse news, in the shape of proofs that the hostile British had allied themselves with the Indians. This was the hardest blow of all for a far-off and feeble settlement, for it might be now swept out of existence almost without a struggle. When the savages were left to resist the advancing white settlers alone, the latter could well flatter themselves that they had some small chance of carrying their point in the end; but to form an union with the armies of a powerful nation like Great Britain, was to give them a strength to which the handful of settlers could offer but a feeble resistance indeed.

Not long after Col. Henderson arrived out among the settlers, he set in operation the plans long matured in his mind. He very well knew that his project of founding a new colony under the title of Transylvania, was an experiment that would prove distasteful to Governor Dunmore, of Virginia, and he therefore made all haste to give it such a shape and form as would put it out of the Governor's power to successfully interfere with its fortunes. To this end, a land-office was speedily opened, where upwards of half a million acres were entered in a short space of time, and titles were issued from the office to settlers in the name of "The Proprietors of the Colony of Transylvania, in America." It was likewise stipulated, in these new titles, that a certain portion of the rents of lands should be held in reservation for the proprietors of the colony, perpetually. There would have been a great deal of trouble with these rents, in time, had the colony kept its original form and character; but when it had performed the work for which it came into existence, it was superseded by better arrangements.

Henderson saw how necessary it was to set up political authority, or at least the show of it, against that of Virginia; such a step would both impart dignity and character to the new project, and inspire the settlers themselves with greater confidence in its reality and success. There were by this time four settlements. Henderson threw himself on his dignity, styled himself the President of the colony, and formally convened a Legislature. This was the first legislative body ever held in the western country. Its members represented an immense territory, though but a trifling constituency. Every one of them was, of necessity, taken from a stockade fort; there were no other collections of houses, or cabins, anywhere in the vast tract they had set out to subdue and populate.

President Henderson called on them, in his proclamation, to meet and form a State. The delegates met in the log fort at Boonesborough, agreeably to the call, on the 23d day of May, 1775. Of the list of members sent from Boonesborough — itself one, and the chief, of the four settlements — Daniel Boone stood naturally at the head. The people all had confidence in him, whether as a leader or a legislator. His brother, Squire Boone, was also a member of this first legislative body, and so was Col. Callaway. These three men were well-tried, and friends in the strongest sense. The Legislature was convened within the fort, which thus became the capitol of the vast territory. Boone was one of the most marked men in the whole body; but John Floyd, who was sent from another settlement, was hardly less so. The latter was of excellent figure, tall and slim, with a dark complexion, and eyes of a peculiar and powerful expression; he was esteemed, in the highest sense, a true Virginia gentleman.

The first act, on opening this legislative body within the walls of the fort, was to offer prayer, asking the blessing of heaven on so great an undertaking. Rev. John Lythe officiated. The scene must have been a solemn and impressive one to the minds of all present. A mere handful of men, assembled in the heart of a scowling wilderness—Indians compassing them around, on this side and that—the Governor of the colony out of which they came hostile to their scheme—and the powerful British Government just lifting its hand to smite them as a feeble settlement had not been smitten before: it is not to be denied that every man of them felt the need of some mighty arm to stay them in an hour like that, and that they fervently sent up their hearts' supplication for divine sympathy and assistance.

It is somewhat remarkable, the style and spirit of the Address sent in to this raw assembly by President Henderson. He tells them that he well understands how small the population is which they represent,— numbering not more than one hundred and fifty in all, but he assured them that they are laying the foundation for an edifice that may endure for all time. And he likewise showed himself a true democrat, in his speech, when alluding to the real source of all power; for, says he, "if any doubt remain among you with respect to the force and efficiency of whatever laws you now or hereafter make, be pleased to consider that *all power is originally in the people;* make it their interest, therefore, by impartial and beneficent laws, and you may be sure of their inclination to see them enforced." The Declaration of Independence, written and subscribed to the following year, contained precisely the same popular spirit.

Gov. Dunmore, of course, opposed the doings of this Transylvania Colony with all the power he could; but his opposition was comparatively very slight, in consequence of the troubles that surrounded him at home. The Governor did fulminate a proclamation, or something of that sort, against them, but it produced no visible effect; the settlers themselves did not care for it, and the Indians, as they well knew, could not understand it. To this proclamation Col. Henderson boldly replied, saying that the "character of his settlers would derive little advantage" from comparison even with that of the Governor himself! And Henderson then makes a shrewd appeal to the selfish interest of the men around him; he speaks quite strongly of "the wanton destruction of our game, the only support of life among many of us, and for want of which the country would be abandoned ere to-morrow, and scarcely a probability remain of its ever becoming the habitation of any Christian people." The Legislature voted a reply to the President's address; the substance of which was, that they had a perfect right to pass laws for their own safety and convenience, and that every colony had the same right of self-government. This was the assertion of genuine democracy, even in the wilds of Kentucky.

Daniel Boone, as a legislator, did his part along with the rest. The particular subject to which he was attracted, was the preservation of game for those who chose to hunt for it; and on the very first day of the session he introduced a bill for the better preserving of game, and was himself made chairman of the committee to which it was referred. He also proposed a measure for improving the breed of horses; and its results may be seen everywhere in Kentucky to this day.

The little Legislature likewise had tender regard for its dignity. One of the men in the fort, named John Guess, having offered a wanton insult to Col. Callaway, the sergeant-at-arms was ordered to bring the offender into the presence of the assembly for proper discipline, and to be made an example of. Besides this, a law was passed making it punishable for a person to practise profane swearing or sabbath-breaking; these backwoods settlers were as exact almost as the Puritans, whose rigid sentiments and customs suggest only the loftiest and most unbending morality.

Three short days sufficed for the sitting of the assembly. The men who composed the body had work to do elsewhere, and they knew better than to fool away their time after the manner of legislators in these modern days. Having enacted such laws as they thought the condition of the new society demanded, they broke up their sitting, and each man went his own way. Prayer, however, was offered by the clergyman when they rose, as when they commenced their brief session. This was a model little Legislature. Its influence on the other settlements became visible forthwith. A platform, as it were, had been erected, and all seemed glad to have it to stand on. The very statement of their political and social principles, however simply and unpretendingly made, would strengthen them all in their new position, and hold them more firmly together as a settlement.

The momentous year, 1776, was now dawning. For the fortunes of the North American Continent it was full of significance. Early this year, the family of Col. Callaway emigrated, and were gladly received into the fort at Boonesborough. There were two young daughters, besides the mother. The family of Col. Benjamin Logan also came out from Virginia, and settled at Logan's Fort. Thus woman's gentle influence was working in favor of the permanence of these frontier settlements, and beginning to hallow the rude scenes of a life in the woods. The beautiful season of spring came and went, covering the plains and prairies with flowers without number. Then the heats of summer began to make themselves felt, and the forest showed the usual signs of the solstitial seasons. There were no orchards, or gardens, planted around them then, and hence the advance of the summer did not betray itself to their eyes by the wilting of leaves, the ripening of vegetables, or the gradual swelling of fruits; nothing but the great forest, whose depths no human eye could penetrate, made signals of the passage of the year.

A circumstance transpired on the 14th of July, of this year, that caused a great excitement throughout the settlement. The narrative has already been well given by Mr. Peck, in his sketch of Boone's life, drawn from the statement of John Floyd, and from sources additional; and we prefer to give it in the words of Mr. Peck himself: —

On the 14th of July, 1776, Betsey Callaway, her sister Frances, and Jemima Boone, a daughter of Capt. Boone, the two last about fourteen years of age, carelessly crossed the river opposite to Boonesborough in a canoe, at a late hour in the afternoon. The trees and shrubs on the opposite bank were thick, and came down to the water's edge. The girls, unconscious of danger, were playing and splashing the water with the paddles, until the canoe, floating with the current, drifted near the shore. Five stout Indians lay there concealed; one of whom, noiseless and stealthy as the serpent, crawling down the bank until he reached the rope that hung from the bow, turned its course up the stream, and in a direction to be hidden from the fort. The loud shrieks of the captured girls were heard, but too late for their rescue. The canoe, their only means of crossing, was on the opposite shore, and none dared to risk the chance of swimming the river, under the impression that a large body of savages was concealed in the woods.

"Boone and Callaway were both absent, and night set in before their return and arrangements could be made for pursuit. Next morning, by daylight, we were on the track, but found they had totally prevented our following them, by walking some distance apart through the thickest canes they could find. We observed their course, and on which side we had left their sign, and travelled upwards of thirty miles. We then imagined that they would be less cautious in travelling, and made a turn in order to cross their trace, and had gone but a few miles before we found their tracks in a buffalo path; pursued and overtook them on going about ten miles, just as they were kindling a fire to cook.

"Our study had been more to get the prisoners, without giving the Indians time to murder them after they discovered us, than to kill them. We discovered each other nearly at the same time. Four of us fired, and all rushed on them, which prevented them from carrying away anything except one shot-gun, without ammunition. Mr. Boone and myself had a pretty fair shot, just as they began to move off. I am well convinced I shot one through, and the one he shot dropped his gun; mine had none. The place was very thick with canes, and being so much elated on recovering the three little broken-hearted girls, prevented our making further search. We sent them off without their moccasins, and not one of them with so much as a knife or a tomahawk."

In the "Life of Boone," by Filson, who represents that he took down every item from the lips of the great pioneer, this incident — so characteristic of the father and the man, and so well calculated to show forth the leading traits of his nature — is disposed of in a very few lines. He merely says that two of Col. Callaway's daughters and one of his own were taken prisoners, near the fort; that he at once set out in pursuit of the Indians, with only eight men; that, after a pusuit of two days, he and his party overtook them, killed two of them, and recovered the girls. It is a meagre story, and undeserving of the character and deeds of the forest monarch whose life it so fairly illustrates.

It so happened — or else it was so arranged beforehand — that on this very same 14th of July on which the three young girls were stolen from the vicinity of the fort, the Indians all around had divided their forces into distinct parties, and determined to make a series of attacks on the different settlements, whenever, and as often, as circumstances would allow. They beheld the increase of the white numbers with great jealousy. They dreaded, too, the protection the forts gave them. If they could be allowed to fight on their own ground, and in their own way, it would all be to their advantage; but this placing the whites under cover was something they could not understand. These attacks were kept up from that time forward, with great regularity. No day was free from suspicion that the Indians were close at hand; no night was so calm and quiet that all slept in their beds without dreams of a stealthy foe in their midst, with tomahawk and scalping-knife brandished above their heads.

At no time in the progress of the settlement of Kentucky, did the scales of her existence as a colony hang so evenly balanced. A feather on this side or that might have changed the result. It is to be confessed that nothing but the protection of an Almighty Power saved it from total destruction. The presence of a man like Daniel Boone upon the field of action, at a critical time like that, was certainly providential; with his thorough knowledge of the Indian character, with his perfect familiarity with the life of the backwoodsman, and, above all, with his cool courage and indomitable perseverance, it is not to be denied that the new colony must inevitably have gone to pieces, truly dissolved in the ferment of the times, but for his presence in the midst of its members. When dangers pressed most closely around them, Boone was ready at hand to extricate them; but when, as now and then was the case, fears of danger were somewhat allayed, no man could appear less intrusive or more modest than he.

It was very difficult, under all the circumstances, for Col. Henderson to obtain *bona fide* purchasers for his lands. Settlers could not be found in plenty, when, in addition to the precarious nature of the title, there was the great danger of being cut off in an unseen hour by the savage. Very little could be offered them by way of inducement to come out and cultivate, or even to purchase, the Transylvania lands. A man could not be out plowing, but a bullet from the Indian whizzed by his ear, discharged from an unseen quarter. If he secured his over-worked and weary cattle at night, it was to find that they had been shot or stolen before the morning. He worked in doubt and danger constantly. Every crackling of the boughs started new fears in his heart. He felt security at no hour, in no place. The peaceful pursuits of agriculture were attended with nearly as much danger and anxiety as war itself.

Then, too, the alliance of the British with the Indians, at this critical juncture — a measure that was freely and indignantly condemned at the time by the best minds in the English Parliament — wrought powerfully against the fortunes of this frontier settlement. This movement on the part of the enemies of the Americans, so bloody and barbarous in its results, could not but infuse new courage into the heart of the red man; he felt now that he had a powerful friend at his back, and that he might dispute the occupation of the forest with the newly-come colonist, with a certain hope of success. There is no telling how much encouragement to resist the peaceful white settler the conduct of the British ministry lent the tribes of western Indians, at this particular time. To add to the embarassment and danger of the hour, numbers of the settlers left again for Virginia, unwilling to endure the constant alarms that were sounded at every hour both of the night and day. Only the brave fellows stayed behind; those who, having once taken hold of the plough, are not in the habit of turning their backs upon their undertaking.

Of all the places at which the Indian aimed his hatred, the Boonsborough Fort was the chief. Here he thought the whole white power was centered. Here, too, his British companions-in-arms taught him to look for the greatest danger to his rule and his land. Hence he watched every moment in its vicinity with a wily temper indeed. Whenever he could find the occupants of the fort in the least degree exposed, he did not fail to make his cruelty felt and remembered.

It was a long and gloomy winter to the Transylvania colonists, this of 1775 and '76. The story was now an old one, that the enmity existing between the colonies and the old country had become permanent and irreconcilable. One side was only struggling for an independent existence, and the other for an iron supremacy. In their loneliness, the handful of brave men who remained to defend the forts, found it exceedingly difficult to pass away the time contentedly. They were obliged, however, to occupy themselves chiefly with watching against assaults of the enemy, and providing for the worst contingencies that might arise. The state of things along the Atlantic coast was truly lamentable; in the far-off wilderness it was scarcely less so. Yet there was one man who bravely stood his ground, let the clouds gather never so densely; and his lofty hopefulness, as well as his steady and reliable courage, lifted up the rest as by main strength. It is not necessary to say that that man was Daniel Boone. From so early a day he had learned the lesson of relying on himself, that he could not be disheartened or discouraged with all the world combined against him. There were great men rising above the heads and shoulders of the people at the East, but none eclipsed him for that serene and benignant greatness which sheds a peaceful lustre all around its path. It was manifestly in the distinct design of Providence, that while the men along the Atlantic border were uniting in a giant effort to repel the tide of foreign oppression, there should be at least *one* true man on the extreme West, in the very heart of the wilderness, too, who was working just as nobly and effectively for the spread of the same freedom which his brethren were defending at the East.

The numbers at the fort were fast getting thinned out; others did not come to supply their places, as was expected. With the troubles at home that engaged their attention, they thought but little of going out into a wilderness to encounter more. It was well known to the Indians, also, that there were fewer white men at the fort during the winter than usual, and they therefore grew bolder every day, coming closer and watching the movements of the garrison more narrowly; so that it was all a man's life was worth, to go outside the enclosure, whether armed or unarmed. Numerous encounters took place near the settlement, in the course of the winter; which General George R. Clarke — a remarkable man, who had just been commissioned to go out against the Indians — noted briefly in his military journal, thus: —

"Dec. 25.— Ten men, going to the Ohio for powder, met on the waters of the Licking Creek by Indians, and defeated. John G. Jones, William Graden and Josiah Dixon were killed.

"Dec. 29.— A large party of Indians attacked McClelland's Fort, and wounded John McClelland, Charles White, Robert Todd, and Edward Worthington, — the two first mortally.

"Dec. 30.— Charles White died of his wound.

"Jan. 6. '77.— John McClelland died of his wound.

"MARCH 5.— Thomas Shores and William Ray killed at the Shawanese spring The Indians attempted to cut off from the fort a small party of our men; a skirmish ensued; we had four men wounded, and some cattle killed. A small party of Indians attacked, killed, and scalped Hugh Wilson. A large party of Indians attacked the stragglers about the fort."

This is about the substance of the winter's experiences. It was nothing but a series of surprises and butcheries, of alarms and murders. No hope was extended the lonely settlers by their friends in Virginia and North Carolina, for the sky was gloomy enough for them at home. Many despaired of the future, believing their prospects of success in those wilds utterly worthless. They thought sorrowfully of their wives and families, left behind in the old colony, and many a time wished themselves secure in the homes from which they had departed. And no man of them loved wife or children more fondly than Boone; yet, through all the darkest trials of the time, and in the midst of the most appalling dangers, he stood steadfast and calm, resting on that sure and lofty hope that always shed its light over his soul.

CHAPTER VII.

BATTLES AND SIEGES.

THERE were but three forts in Kentucky, at the time of which we are speaking; that at Boonesborough, which was the most important one, — that at Harrodsburgh, — and what was known as Logan's Fort. At Boonesborough there was a garrison of but twenty-two men; at Logan's Fort of only fifteen; and Harrodsburgh held sixty-five, — more than both the others together. That is, there were only one hundred and two men to hold the entire frontier against the assaults of Indians and British combined; and by the treaties that had been formed between the latter and the former, it was easy for a mixed army to be precipitated upon this little handful of settlers from the line of posts along to the north, that would crush them out of existence. It is said that about three hundred of the settlers had gone back to Virginia again, either disheartened at the prospects, or grown too timid to remain and hold their position. This of course entailed more severe service on the few who remained at their post; they were on the watch continually;

all had to take their turns, and take them pretty often, too.

At this juncture, those troubles that had been growing between the government of Virginia and the Transylvania Colony, came to a head. The crisis was brought on by the over-anxiety of the settlers to establish the title to their lands. Somehow the impression was becoming general that Col. Henderson could not hold the tract he had been parcelling out to the rest, except perhaps against the Indians; and that the Virginia government would at last step in and claim the rights that were vested in itself as the primary owner and disposer of the whole.

The truth was, there were two parties in this matter; the settlers from North Carolina were of Scotch descent, and had a feeling of devotion to their leader above all others, — while those from Virginia believed only in the supremacy of their own government. Virginia, too, had long looked with jealous watchfulness upon a man like Henderson, who had the boldness to set up a separate government of his own, calling himself the head, or President; nor was it at all to her liking that he took it upon himself to parcel out valuable tracts of land to whose title she made sole claim, and property in which she was resolved should be dispensed only through her. By her charter, obtained from the British Government, Virginia laid claim to the whole of Kentucky, and neither Col. Henderson, nor any other man, could successfully deprive her of her royal inheritance. Seeing how matters stood between the proprietors of Transylvania and the government of Virginia, a great many of those who had occupied lands were naturally undecided which side to take; while party feeling, on the other hand, began to rage to an extent that foreboded nothing but danger.

Fortunately, however, either through the commanding influence of Henderson himself, or in consequence of the feeling that such a man deserved at least a testimonial of public gratitude for the services he had performed, while Virginia openly declared his title to the lands null and void, she made a compromise by which his individual claim was asserted to be good against the Indian owners; and he was afterwards presented with a grant twelve miles square, located on the Ohio. Boone hated and despised all these men who had come out from the mother colonies for the sake of speculating in lands; and the extreme anxiety betrayed by many about their titles, disgusted him with the conduct of men whose selfish interests alone governed them. These troubles, added to those occasioned by the Indians, were enough to dishearten any but a thoroughly brave and hopeful man. A large portion of the settlers signed and forwarded a petition to the authorities of Virginia. which was called, "A petition of the inhabitants, and some of the intended settlers, of that part of North America, now denominated Transylvania;" the object of the same being to express their continued attachment to the government of the parent colony, to set forth the deceit that had been practised upon them by Col. Henderson and the other self-styled proprietors of the lands, and to declare that the lands still belonged, in their judgment, to his majesty, the King of England; and that they were, as heretofore, his true and loyal subjects. One passage in the petition we quote, as best showing the spirit of the whole:—

"And, as we have the greatest reason to presume that his majesty, to whom the lands were deeded by the Six Nations for a valuable consideration, will vindicate his title, and think himself at liberty to grant them to such persons and on such terms as he pleases, your petitioners would, in consequence thereof, be turned out of possession, or obliged to purchase their lands and improvements on such terms as the new grantee or proprietor might think fit to impose ; so that we cannot help regarding the demands of Mr. Henderson and company as highly unjust and impolitic in the infant state of the settlement, as well as greatly injurious to your petitioners, who would caerfully have paid the consideration at first stipulated by the company whenever their grant had been confirmed by the crown, or otherwise authenticated by the Supreme Legislature."

They therefore " humbly expect and implore " to be taken under the protection of the Colony of Virginia, and beseech its interposition in their behalf, that they may not be made sufferers by the imposition of the gentlemen styling themselves proprietors, who, " the better to effect their oppressive designs, have given them the color of a law, enacted by a score of men, *artfully picked from the few adventurers* who went to see the country last summer, overawed by the presence of Mr. Henderson."

Virginia, through her Supreme Legislature, declared that the titles of the Transylvania Company were null and void, and the colony vanished, as a colony, into thin air at once. And thus ended the plan of the settlement in Kentucky known by the name of Transylvania.

There was by this time a concerted movement

BATTLES AND SIEGES. 127

among the savages to make a descent on the fort at Boonesborough; they had waited and watched to see what the great strength of the pioneers consisted in, and now, having perfectly satisfied themselves, they resolved to surround the whites in a body and endeavor to destroy them. The garrison at Boonesborough was exceedingly small; the Indians came down upon them in numbers exceeding one hundred. Of course there was dangerous odds against the whites. They made their attack on the 15th of April. It was a sudden and terrible one. Their savage natures had been aroused to the highest pitch of excitement. They dashed, like waves upon rocks, against the feeble enclosure of the settlers in the wilderness. The forest rang again with their shrill shouts and cries. Their lithe and dusky forms peopled the solitudes as the white men had never seen them peopled before. They came on with the yells of infuriated beasts, striking terror into the hearts of all who heard them.

It appeared, for a time, as if the little fort was much too frail to withstand the wild onset. They behaved as if nothing could keep them from pouring in a living stream into the fort, and visiting the little garrison with a general massacre. The white settlers made sorry work among them with their unerring rifles. How many of the savages were thus picked off was never known; for they were careful to conceal their losses by carrying off their dead and wounded. Yet it was believed, with good reason, that they were sore sufferers. Their unexpected losses served to make them still more ferocious. They raved and stormed against the entrenched garrison with the fury of desperation. But it was to no purpose. The skill and coolness of the white man were more than a match for the Indian.

They sullenly turned their backs, therefore, and plunged into the shadows of the wilderness. Now they knew what it was to meet the fire of the brave white settlers. It must have tasked them still more to bear their dead away with them, especially when so sorely fatigued with the results of a vain and bloody assault against a determined foe. That, however, was their usual practise, which they would have followed in the present case if it had cost every one of them his life. The evidences of the desperate combat were all around the locality. The garrison to be sure, did not lose but a single man, which was a very slight misfortune for them, under such threatening circumstances.

They must have thought themselves fortunate to have remained masters of their position.

The savages were not satisfied with this; it only whetted their appetite for more. Like the wolf, having once tasted blood, they would follow up their ferocious instincts wherever they led them. The men within the fort looked for a speedy renewal of the attack, nor were they disappointed in their expectations. The Indians came out of the forest in dense and dark legions, on the 4th of July. They numbered a larger mass than ever. They came and sat down before the rude fortress as for a regular siege, resolved either to fight or starve their determined enemy out. The numbers stood about two hundred Indians to one white man; overwhelming odds, truly, and apparently discouraging.

For forty-eight hours the savages kept up the siege. Every white man's head that was exposed in the least, was during that period in imminent danger. They howled and shrieked, they whooped and yelled in their barbarous frenzy, expecting that the deadly terror they would thus strike into the hearts of the white men within the fort would somehow lead to their easier overthrow. The wild beasts themselves, coming from their forest lairs, could not have made night more hideous than did these Indians, with their unearthly yells and cries. Those within the fortress, however, were not inspired with terror, but rather with desperation. Too well they knew that this was their last chance to hold or lose all — and they might the latter. The fighting between the opposing parties, during the time the place was thus besieged by the Indians, was as close as any that had yet occured. The little garrison came off, however, with the loss of but a single man, as in the previous contest; fewer were wounded, too, than before. The courage of Daniel Boone in this encounter was especially conspicuous; he dared all that any brave man could dare, and exercised a wariness that made him an equal match even for the Indian.

Soon after this, other settlers began to come into the forts, and were received with manifestations of the greatest joy. When a garrison was reduced to the dimensions of this, the slightest accession to its numbers could not but be hailed with delight. Forty-five men arrived from North Carolina, in the last week of July, and a hundred more came from Virginia in the latter part of August; making an accession of valuable men to the settlement really worth speaking of. All along through the summer and into the autumn, they continued to have skirmishes with the Indians, but they always came out best from each encounter. There was no end, apparently, to the ingenuity practised by the savage in selecting the time and mode of his attacks. At any hour of the day, he was liable to beset the party of white men hunting in the forest; and through the still night hours there was no cessation from fears of his presence.

Boone was wary and watchful. The red man himself was not more than a match for him in that respect. And in addition to this trait of caution and judgment, he possessed all the attributes of the highest courage. No mere military man could inspire followers with deeper confidence than he. He never hesitated to lead wherever any dared to follow. Still with all his rough experience with the savage, calculated, one would suppose, to harden his finer feelings and check the growth of his nobler nature, Daniel Boone never became infected with the atmosphere of his surroundings of cruelty; he was just as ready to perform acts requiring personal sacrifice, as ever; he lost none of that sweetness, and simplicity, and truth which made his character the fresh and peculiar one it was. And that is saying much for the man who was exposed and tried as Boone was.

As the Revolutionary struggle progressed, and the distance between the old thirteen colonies and the mother country became greater and greater, the settlers on the western frontier were made to feel more keenly the suffering with which the British power was able to visit them. That power held in its grasp the ferocious impulses and revengeful inclinations of a vast horde of savages, scattered all along the line of the western waters, and could at any time give them free rein to murder and devastate after their own peculiarly cruel methods. Nor did it scruple to employ these means, oftentimes making such work as caused a shudder of horror in the hearts of those at home who read the bloody tales.

A man now appeared upon the field, who was destined to play a brilliant and important part in the early history of the western country. His name was George R. Clarke. No greater military man has ever associated his name with the annals of our early western settlements. As a brave man, he had long been familliarly known in the old Virginia colony, and he enjoyed the confidence of Lord Dunmore, the royal Governor, in a marked degree. The latter had even offered him a military commission under British authority, but that he had nobly declined. He was a patriot by nature, and the only country he had learned to love was that on whose generous soil he was born.

At once on the occurence of the crisis in the affairs of Transylvania, he came forward and assumed the authority and influence which belonged to him by nature. He was of the opinion that the claims to land, derived from Col. Henderson, would not stand against the claims of Virginia; and his personal influence went so far as to convince the most of the settlers that his opinion on the subject was the only correct one. Therefore, when the settlers petitioned the Government of Virginia to take them under its protection, they united in sending General Clarke to present their request, and to represent all their wishes and interests. The Virginia Council for a long time hesitated. They were asked to furnish the settlers with five hundred weight of powder, in case the latter should require it, in their defence against the Henderson party. But the Council were undecided whether they would be able to make a successful resistance against that party, in the event of an outbreak, or would be overwhelmed by them in their turn; in the latter case, the powder would only be lost, which, at that particular crisis, the Virginia colony could ill afford; nor, indeed, did it wish to precipitate a quarrel with a strong party of frontiersmen, led by such a captain as Henderson.

Still, they were forced to listen to the appeals of these settlers, in time, especially when their danger from the combined forces of the British and Indians was presented in such vivid colors. Unless the men on the frontier were aided very soon, they would be swept under by the engulfing wave whose crest was already raised over their heads. Gen. Clarke talked very plainly to them, telling them that "a country not worth defending was not worth claiming." This latter argument appeared conclusive with them. He returned to Kentucky invested with large military authority, and proceeded at once to block out operations.

There were three important garrisons on the north western frontier, that were occupied by the British and Indians—at Detroit, Vincennes, and Kaskaskias. The young reader who is not familiar with their location, will do well to make himself acquainted with the same by referring to the map. Clarke said that there was but one way by which to intimidate the savage, and that was by striking a vigorous and decisive blow at once. He therefore resolved to make a concerted attack on each of these three fortresses, surprising the garrison perhaps into a surrender. He wanted bold men to work with him. He looked around to find those, who, while as cautious and wary as the Indian himself, were still as fearless as lions to go out into an encounter.

While in Virginia, he laid his plans before the leading men of the State, including Wythe, and Jefferson, and Henry — all of the greatest minds the Old Dominion ever produced. They encouraged it, and he felt new strength and resolution to proceed. As soon as he got back to the west again, he set about making his arrangements to invest these well-equipped forts. He found the men who were ready to go with him and perform the work. Of these men, Daniel Boone stood foremost and first. On him he felt that he could rely. The man who had already gone successfully through two regular sieges at the hands of the Indians that swarmed in the wilderness, could not be the wrong one to clothe wich authority in an undertaking like this. Boone, too, understood the nature and ways of the Indian. He was cool and sagacious. Having already fought the savage, he knew his mode of warfare, and could turn such knowledge to ready account.

The enemy had not, by any means, either, been careful hitherto to keep quiet within the lines he had established for himself; on the contrary, the practise was to make continual irruptions on the peaceful settlers, surprising them when engaged in planting or sowing their seed, watching the chances to pick them off when out in the forest hunting for game, and managing to harass and keep them in perpetual fear, in every possible way. It had come to so dangerous a pass, that each settler was obliged to go out like an armory, his hunting-knife in his belt, his unerring rifle across his shoulder, and barely sufficient subsistence in his pouch to keep him alive to do the work he went forth to do. If he strolled a rod away from the fort where he belonged, he felt that he might be the perpetual target for an Indian lurking in the shadow of some tree. Hence the war was of a predatory character, each one for himself, and no hour safe from the probabilities of an attack.

If the savages, too, felt an intense degree of hatred against the great fort at Boonesborough, which had so far stood its ground against all assaults, they felt no less respect and fear for the white man from whom it took its name. He was almost like the Great Spirit in their eyes. No other leader among the pale-faces ever inspired his forest enemies with such reverence; they knew that he was not cruel and vindictive, like some of them, though there is no reason why, after the murder of his son by the Indians, he should not have a heart as full of passion and revenge as the rest; and there was something in his very presence withal, that impressed his character on their imaginations with the depth and strength of a being much above the mortal.

The first thing done by Gen. Clarke was to select and organize a board of forest-rangers, or spies, who could track their solitary way in the deep wilderness, hover on the outskirts of the enemy, and fetch and carry reports with the utmost promptness and reliability. The payment for their services it was pledged by Clarke should be made by Virginia. All along the Ohio banks they travelled, taking their lives in their hands. The men of our time can have no conception of the perils with which they were environed. Clad in their hunting toggery — mocassins, buckskin breeches, and a hunter's shirt of leather, and armed with the keen knife and inseparable rifle, they plunged into dense growths of forest, and tracked paths through the close-serried ranks of the cane, with the same sense of security with which the savage trod those wilds himself. The work to be done by the spy, therefore, courageous as it was in the largest sense, was attended with a great deal more danger on the western frontier, than within range of the enemy's sentinels on the Atlantic border.

Prominent among all brave and memorable western scouts, or spies, is the name of Simon Kenton. He performed a vast deal of invaluable work at this particular juncture. There was a secret cause for his thus taking to the perils and excitements of a spy among the Indian forts, which deserves narration. Boone made choice of him immediately, confiding to him some of his deepest projects for the reduction of the enemy's fortresses and the defence of his own. Of a more sincere and beautiful friendship than that which existed between Boone and Kenton, the history of no early state, east or west, furnishes any example. The name of Simon Kenton — or Simon Butler, as it came to be — is indissolubly associated with that of Boone all over the west. Boone's choice of the man for the service required, showed the deepest insight on the part of the great Pioneer.

Kenton, early in life, was deeply in love with a young woman, who failed to return his passion. She preferred another beau to him. This was more than the hot blood of the young man could endure. When his lady-love called her friends together to witness the ceremony of her marriage, Simon Kenton was present, uninvited; he did not care to be invited; he could witness that ceremony without going through a needless form of that kind. Of course his presence created much excitement in the bridal party, and, in the custom of those rude times, there was a tussle between the successful and unsuccessful young man, which resulted rather in the latter's discomfiture. He vowed vengeance, however, and watched his opportunity. It was not long in coming round. The two young fellows met. Kenton got the better of his adversary, and used him savagely. Supposing he had taken his life, he fled for the shelter of the forest. Changing his name to that of Simon Butler, he entered on a life of wild excitement and reckless daring, which could be desired by no living mortal except, perhaps, to keep down internal excitements immeasurably stronger and deeper. There are a great many stories told, throughout the west, of his extreme sufferings in certain cases, when he fell into the hands of the Indians. It is said that he was eight times compelled to run the gauntlet, which was no slight undertaking, nor holding out many chances of escape finally; he was three times fastened to the stake; and once he came very near being sacrificed by a blow from an axe, or tomahawk. He stole a horse from the Indians once, and they not long afterwards caught him; and the following account shows what kind of treatment he received from the moment he became a captive: — "After beating him till their arms were too tired to indulge that gratifying recreation any longer, they secured him for the night. This was done by first placing him upon his back to the ground. A pole was then laid across his breast, and his hands tied to each end, and his arms lashed with thongs around it, the thongs passing under his body so as to keep the pole stationary. After all this, another thong was passed around his neck, and the end of it secured to a stake in the ground, his head being stretched back so as not entirely to choke him. In this original manner he was left to pass the night."

CHAPTER VIII.

A PRISONER.

MORE than once, Simon Kenton was instrumental in saving Boone's life. Kenton was on the watch, one day, standing at the gate of the fort. He was about going forth on the service of a spy. His rifle was loaded, and he was otherwise equipped for his work. It was quite early in the morning. A couple of men belonging to the fort were out in the fields not far off, engaged in hoeing. Suddenly Kenton observed that the men were fired upon. He knew instantly that Indians were at hand. Finding themselves unhurt, the two men started and ran with all speed for the fort. The savages followed as rapidly. One of the poor fellows was overtaken within a few rods of the fort, and tomahawked in sight of Kenton himself. The latter put his rifle to his shoulder, drew the trigger, and the savage who had done the deed fell dead in his tracks. Revenge was in swift pursuit.

The Indians were very bold in approaching so near; but they had learned not to fear the white man, from familiarity with his presence. Furthermore, they were there in such strength that the risk they run was slight indeed. Boone was within the fort at the time Kenton fired his rifle with such effect at the Indian. The sound was an alarm for his practised ear, and, with ten trusty men, he started off after the savages. The latter did not run, but seemed inclined to stand their ground. Boone and his little party were speedily fighting in the midst of them. Kenton's quick eye saw one savage in the act of taking deadly aim at Boone himself, and he shot him dead on the spot, before his bullet could perform its fatal errand.

So sudden was the alarm — it being at an early hour of the morning, too — that Boone had thought only of making an instantaneous sally and driving the invaders off with a dash; he had not stopped to calculate in how large force they might be, nor what were the chances of his coming off victorious. He was struck aback with surprise, therefore, to find himself and his ten followers completely surrounded! The hostile Indians had managed to place themselves in considerable numbers between him and the fort! There was but one way by which he might save himself, and that was by rushing first upon open destruction. He made a rush — such as only men like him ever dare to attempt — calling out to his followers to fire upon the red-skins, and plunge into their ranks. They did as they were ordered; and, but for the deadly fire of the Indians themselves, who were prepared to resist such an onset, they would have cut their way through safely and successfully. The Indians fired simultaneously with the rush the party made at them. Boone himself was wounded, and fell to the ground. Six others, also, received bullets from the savages' guns. An Indian at once dashed forward as the white men fell, and raised his tomahawk to knock out the brains of the prostrate Pioneer; but the keen eye of Kenton was upon him, and an unerring ball followed the course of the eye in a twinkling. Down came the Indian to the ground, biting the dust in the agony of death. Kenton was proving himself invaluable. Boone was carried into the fort with his leg broken; the rest were also got in with great haste, and then the gates were shut fast against the foe. The Pioneer never forgot the obligations he owed to his generous preserver. It is true, he could not give them expression, yet they lived none the less deeply in his large and noble heart.

This is but one of the many similar scenes that were enacted at that time on the frontiers of Kentucky. There was hardly any life but that which comprised alarms and surprises. All labor outside the fort was performed only under the protection of well armed guards, and at particular hours of the day. The land was held at the greatest possible cost, both of labor and endurance. Men slept on their rifles. They did not stir out without them. A watchful guard had to be kept all the time, lest a wily red fellow might by some chance stealthily creep up and surprise them. There were skirmishes, too, continually. Scarcely a week passed over, without one or more of them.

The life at the fort would be deeply interesting, if it could only be told in minute detail, just as it was. We know that Boone was a silent man by habit, thoughtful, and disposed, even when he did talk, to say what he wished in few words, and meaning ones. It may readily be imagined, therefore, with what a silent interest he would listen to the reports of the scouts and spies as they came in from their tramps in the forest, telling what they had discovered in relation to the Indians or British. He would sit and work over his rifle, treating it with as much tenderness as if it had been his own child. They would tell of Indians they had spied, prowling about in this quarter or that, and the Pioneer's eyes would instantly kindle with a new fire. Or he would hear their reports of some trail upon which they had unexpectedly come, and give their opinions as to where they thought it conducted, or what was the real meaning of it; and his excited countenance spoke more eloquently than words of the active working of his own thoughts. Any story about the Indians caught and held his attention. He was at home on that subject, and continued to make it his chief study. While his wounded leg troubled him, he kept close within the walls of the fort, spending his time in listening to the daily, and sometimes hourly, reports of the scouts that came in, and counselling for measures to be taken against assault and surprises, and going through the process of affectionately cleaning his rifle even when it needed no such attention or care. Sometimes he grew impatient to find that, in the time of greatest need, he was not able to go out and perform that service of which he was once capable; but immediately his old philosophy would return to his mind, and he became content to know that he had escaped even with his life, and that in good time all would be right again.

Then when he got better of his wound, and his strength allowed him to go out as he used to do, it was pleasant to see with what a relish he threaded his way into the wilderness, where it was densest and darkest, watching the bend of every twig and bough, studying the appearance of the long wild-grass, keenly piercing the dim vista to see if it contained moving figures of men, cautiously secreting himself behind a giant tree and watching for possible approaches of the enemy, running his glance like the motion of thought over the masses of cane-brake — impervious to other men's eyes, but full of visible secrets to his — or, perhaps, falling in with some new comers on the road westward to the now well-known fort, and gladly offering to convoy them to the haven where they would desire most ardently to be. One fact was particularly characteristic of him; that he was ready to perform labor that involved large personal sacrifices for others, when he cared little or nothing about doing aught for himself.

Having been shut in for so many months in the fort without the means of making their usual sallies out for provisions of this and that sort, it naturally fell out that the garrison began pretty soon to suffer from the lack of salt. This is a necessary article in the line of subsistence, no one being able for a very long time to live without it, although Boone says of himself that he did, during those long and solitary months when he was left alone in the wilds of Kentucky. The settlers at the fort came to the conclusion that something must be done, and done forthwith. They could not live much longer, at least in a state of comparative health, unless they could procure salt. They well knew of certain places along the course of the streams, where salt was to be had in plenty, the wild beasts of the forest having revealed to them the important secret in the first place. Accordingly an expedition was planned to go out and procure at these places the much needed commodity.

When a measure of this sort was to be taken, Boone was the man all ready to enlist in it. He did in this case; in truth, he it was who most urgently counselled its necessity. A party of men, all abundantly armed, was made up for the expedition. Who should — nay, who *could*, properly command and pilot it, but Daniel Boone himself? The rest instinctively looked up to him as their leader, and would have appeared to follow him, even if some other man had been their nominal captain. Thirty men set forth. They knew full well what they were about to undertake, and went prepared with trusty rifles and stout hearts.

Their destination was to what was known as the Blue Licks, one of the most famous and valuable places for the free production of salt known in Kentucky. To protect this possession, the white settler would willingly have made as great sacrifices as he would to defend the fort itself. There are several springs that make up the Blue Licks, but the largest of them all is situated on the Licking River — so named from the practise of the animals in coming there to *lick* the salt — which, at the present day, lies in Nicholas County, in the northeast corner of Kentucky. There was many a fierce and bloody conflict fought at and near this place, and the entire neighborhood forms one of the most important of all the localities that helped make up, for Kentucky, the title of the "dark and bloody ground."

Splendid hotels, with numerous out-buildings, occupy the spot now, attracting to it the most gay and fashionable of all the pleasure-seekers of the land. It would hardly be recognized as the same spot which originated so many bloody encounters between the white settler and the ferocious red man of the forest.

After a cautious and quite slow march — necessarily so, because of the unseen dangers that lurked everywhere around them — Boone and his brave little band of thirty men arrived in safety, and without the loss of a single one of their number, at the place, and began immediate operations. They set their salt kettles in which to evaporate the water from the spring, and went about the task of manufacturing the salt required for the use of the garrison. It was important that the work should be done with great dispatch, for the moment the Indians found out what they were at, there would come an end to their operations.

Sundry exciting incidents occurred while this little party were at the springs, and among the rest one which our government has thought worthy of preservation in stone, in a sculptured group ornamenting the rotunda of the Capitol at Washington. It is not altogether probable, or it would possess a deeper and truer interest. Evidently the story has been stretched to fit the imaginary character of Boone, instead of being given in the perfectly simple garb of truth. We tell it, however, in the very words it has been told in before : —

"Boone, instead of taking part in the diurnal and uninterrupted labor of evaporating the water, performed the more congenial duty of hunting to keep the company in provisions while they labored. In this pursuit, he had one day wandered some distance from the bank of the river. Two Indians, armed with muskets — for they had now generally added these efficient weapons to their tomahawks — came upon him. His first thought was to retreat. But he discovered, from their nimbleness, that this was impossible. His second thought was resistance, and he slipped behind a tree to await their coming within rifle-shot. He then exposed himself, so as to attract their aim. The foremost leveled his musket. Boone, who could dodge the flash at the pulling of the trigger, dropped behind his tree unhurt. The next object was to cause the fire of the second musket to be thrown away in the same manner. He again exposed part of his person. The eager Indian instantly fired, and Boone evaded the shot, as before. Both the Indians, having thrown away their fire, were eagerly striving, but with trembling hands, to reload. Trepidation and too much haste retarded their object. Boone drew his rifle, and one of them fell dead. The two antagonists, now on equal ground, the one unsheathing his knife and the other poising his tomahawk, rushed toward the dead body of the fallen Indian. Boone, placing his foot on the dead body, dexterously received the well-aimed tomthawk of his powerful enemy on the barrel of his rifle, thus preventing his skull from being cloven by it. In the very attitude of firing, the Indian had exposed his body to the knife of Boone, who plunged it in his body to the hilt."

Whether this narrated incident is strictly true or not, we think there were a great many acts in his exciting experience that better deserve to be preserved in stone, for the instruction and pleasure of future generations. It would make a vivid picture any where; but it is not deeply and radically illustrative of the quality of the great Pioneer's calm and noble nature. It exhibits him merely as more powerful and skillful than the Indian; whereas, it ought to be understood that he had no superior, in his own characteristics, even among *white men.* Read the verses of Byron, to be found in the first chapter, over again.

The party of salt makers remained at the Blue Licks, pursuing their avocations, for about a month. They worked hard, and watched continually, and in all that time they were not once interrupted. Meantime, the Indians had got intelligence of Boone's absence from the fort, and concluded it was the right time to make an attack on the place and capture it. It took them a very little while to make up a party of assailants and come down from the northward to carry out their design. They numbered somewhat over one hundred, and all felt an exulting confidence in their success. On their way to the fort, they came near the very spot where the salt party were encamped. It was now early in the month of February. Boone was out in the forest hunting for those who were at work at the spring. He had failed to see any Indians for so long that he began to believe the danger was chiefly over; men are apt to be careless in such matters at just the moment when there happens to be most need of watchfulness.

This very party, that had been assembled for the capture of the fort, suddenly came upon him while thus alone in the wood. He spied them as soon as they saw him. The danger was imminent. His first swift thought was, How am I to escape? Then seeing the utter impossibility of doing that, his next thought was, What is the best mode of giving myself up? The profoundest sagacity of the experienced hunter was now put to the test. It was a long time since he had been a prisoner in the hands of the Indians, and it was then under very different circumstances, too, from the present ones. It was plain that resistance would be fruitless; he would be certain to lose his life in attempting it; he knew how much better it would be for him to surrender with entire willingness and grace, and how much more it would please the savages, too. Accordingly he made signs to them to let them understand that he was completely in their power, and that he should neither attempt to fly, nor offer resistance.

Approaching them with perfect confidence and self-possession, he extended his hand in token of peaceful surrender. They surrounded him in a moment. He made them understand that he willingly gave himself up to them; they promised him that he should not be harmed, but that the best attentions should be paid him. Thus far, he was easy in his mind.

But he reflected that the party at the spring ought to be provided for.

They ought to be warned against the impending danger. How could it be done? It was out of *his* power to communicate with them, much less to get to them; and it was not less evident to him that, unless he could in some way interpose between his captors and them, the latter must be cut off to a man. It tasked his utmost ingenuity, and called forth all his native coolness, to put his desire in a way of practical accomplishment.

He very well understood that, as matters stood at

that time, the party at the salt licks were sure to be surprised and captured, perhaps murdered; it would be far better, therefore, even to seem timid, or cowardly, than to forego the exercise of every opportunity he might have to save them. The chief merit of his conduct was, under the stress of circumstances, to be looked for in the *result*, not in the exact means employed; especially when those means were so extremely limited.

No time was to be lost. Boone pretended to be perfectly satisfied with his captivity, and his conduct even flattered his captors, leading them to think he truly felt what he only feigned. Besides, he was known to them to be anything but a vindictive and bloodthirsty man, and they could not have laid a single charge of downright cruelty to his account. In brief, it took him a very little time to so work himself into their favor, that he shortly discovered he possessed decided influence over them. That was the happy moment for him to strike, and he failed not to improve it. He requested the Indians to allow him to conduct them to his party of white friends. They consented, of course watching his conduct closely. As they came up to the camp of the salt-boilers, the latter were surprised beyond measure to find their old leader in such company, and, particularly, leading them on; and their astonishment was still more heightened to see that he made signs to them not to offer any resistance to the savages, but to make up their minds to surrender.

In spite of their wonder, however, they were obedient to the signals. They had unlimited confidence in their trusty leader, and would have done almost anything he bade them. Therefore they made no show of resistance. They stood still and allowed themselves to be taken willing captives. Boone had, without doubt, told his captors how much influence he possessed over his men, and they must have been powerfully impressed with some superstitious idea respecting his superiority. They could hardly be made to see how the mere giving of a sign by a single man, and he unarmed and in the power of his foes, could work so mysterious a result on the minds of a party of other men. At any rate, if Boone's friends had not been ready to obey his secret signal, there would have been fought on that spot a bloody battle between the two parties, and it is not easy to say that a single white man would have been left to tell the tale. The men were all carried off by the Indians, and well used as long as they remained prisoners. As Boone had been solemnly promised by the Indians — in case he would prevail on his friends to make no resistance — not one of them was injured.

This piece of conduct on the part of Boone, however, was very severely criticised by some; so much so that when he regained his liberty and returned to the settlements, he was subjected to a formal trial by court-martial. It happened very strangely, too, that his personal friends brought the charges of cowardice and improper conduct against him, — Col. Callaway and Col. Logan. He made a spirited defence, speaking for himself on the matter, and it proved effectual; he was acquitted. Those who had been so ready to charge him with such a crime as that of treachery, or even to impute to him a spirit of cowardice, were now compelled to acknowledge the far-sighted shrewdness shown by him on this trying occasion, and to admit that, under the peculiar circumstances, no man could have acted with more circumspection and prudence. It would have been the easiest thing in the world to risk a battle, and nothing, either, would so completely have secured the annihilation of every white man in the party. A rash man, with cowardly inclinations, would have been quite apt to do just what Boone's superior coolness and sagacity told him was *not* best to be done.

The Indians naturally revolved in their minds what was best to do next. Should they go forward and capture the Boonesborough fort, or should they take their prisoners along with them and proceed through the wilderness to their own entrenchments?

Boone was greatly exercised in his mind to know which they would do, for it was of the first importance; had they attacked the fort, thus deprived of the services of some of its best men, and especially without Boone's presence among the garrison, nothing can be plainer than that the place would have been obliged to capitulate, and the entire body of settlers must have been cut off. The prudent policy of the great Pioneer, however, served to work in their favor, and so it must have appeared afterwards to the more reflecting of them. But in consequence of Boone's perfect truthfulness to them, and remembering that their present captives did not cost them a single life—no, nor even a single shot— they thought less about an enterprise like that of capturing the fort, and believed, if they troubled themselves about it at all, that it could be assailed just as successfully at another time. Here was where the diplomacy of Daniel Boone, as betrayed in the peaceful surrender of his men, is especially to be noted and commended.

All this occurred, it is to be remembered, in the inclement and trying month of February. At such a season as that, too, the prisoners were marched off together to Chillicothe, which was the leading settlement of the Indians in that section.

The journey was made under as comfortable circumstances as could have been expected. The weather was extremely cold, however, and all endured more or less suffering from exposure. The white captives were treated with great leniency, and even with kindness; they admitted that they had nothing to complain of. It could not have been so disheartening to them, either, knowing that their leader was a captive like themselves, ready to share the same hard fortunes or terrible fate, and had also counselled them to surrender as they did.

Thus through the dreary wilderness, in mid winter, they marched. They reached the Indian village in due course of time, without any incident by the way worthy of particular mention. Once received into the savage settlement, they were objects of the liveliest curiosity to all the children of the forest, and were continually surrounded by groups of women and children, anxiously studying their peculiarities of dress and character.

CHAPTER IX.

A WONDERFUL ESCAPE.

DESIROUS of acquainting their white allies, the British, with the results of their prowess, the Indians sent off Boone and ten chosen men of the captured party through the wilderness, and across rivers and creeks, to the British fort at Detroit. General Hamilton was in command at that noted place, and it is charged that, in obedience to the spirit of the alliance then existing between the British and Indians, he had offered large sums of money for all the scalps of the white men that the Indians might bring in. He has the credit, however, of humanely telling the savages that he preferred living prisoners to scalps, which was so much in his favor when sentiments so civilized were not in the fashion.

They were about three weeks in making the journey, which they did with some difficulty. Boone all the while pretended to be contented with his lot, and thus deceived his captors the more. Little is recorded of the journey itself; he is mute respecting it. Arrived at Detroit, he became at once the

A WONDERFUL ESCAPE. 161

observed of all. Hamilton, the British commander, knew much about him, because he could not well help knowing in what esteem he had been held by Gov. Dunmore, of Virginia. The officers and soldiers showed him many personal attentions, which he greatly prized, and repeatedly placed their funds at his disposal. He was escorted around wherever he chose to go in the neighborhood, by his Indian guides, all the while professing himself satisfied with his new fortunes. Hamilton offered the Indians as large a sum as one hundred pounds sterling, or five hundred dollars, for his ransom, but the Indians refused the offer unconditionally. They knew how valuable a prize they had in the person of the Pioneer of Kentucky.

He stayed at Detroit for a month, at no time betraying the least discontent or desire to escape. And when they saw this contentment, even after their prompt refusal to give him up into the hands of the commander of the fort, the savages were more than ever convinced that he was one of themselves, and would ere long assimilate to their customs and habits. He disguised his real feelings admirably — there is no denying it. Their respect for him had now increased many fold. Above all his other characteristics, they liked his steady calmness and persistent silence; these were peculiarly traits of their own. Then, too, he was as brave as the bravest of their own warriors. If they could but secure the alliance and friendship of such a man as that, they considered that wonderful results would have been accomplished. To this end, they were quite willing to leave all to time.

After having made this public exhibition of their distinguished prisoner, the Indians set out on their return to Chillicothe. They left his comrades with the British — himself alone they would not let go, so great a prize was he esteemed in their eyes. The return journey began on the 10th of April, and was continued for a tedious length of time before they finally reached the old Indian village again. Boone's well-trained eyes — through which alone some men educate themselves entirely — observed everything; not a feature of the fine country through which he passed, escaped him. That same section at the present day produces immense wealth for the nation whose boast its possession is.

Arrived at Chillicothe once more, he describes his way of life there, with the help of his biographer's pen, in the following way: —

" At Chillicothe I spent my time as comfortably as I could expect; was adopted, according to their custom, into a family, where I became a son, and had a great share in the affection of my new parents, brothers, sisters and friends. I was exceedingly familiar and friendly with them, always appearing as cheerful and satisfied as possible, and they put great confidence in me. I often went a hunting with them, and frequently gained their applause for my activity at our shooting matches. I was careful not to exceed many of them in shooting, for no people are more envious than they in this sport. I could observe in their countenances and gestures the greatest expressions of joy, when they exceeded me; and, when the reverse happened, of envy. The Shawanese king took great notice of me, and treated me with profound respect and entire friendship, often entrusting me to hunt at my liberty. I frequently returned with the spoils of the woods, and as often presented some of what I had taken to him, expressive of duty to my sovereign. My food and lodging were in common with them; not so good, indeed, as I could desire, but necessity made everything acceptable."

In order to become a member of the tribe, and particularly to be admitted into the family of the chieftain, he was obliged to go through certain ceremonies that must have cost his feelings a large sacrifice; but he considered the object to be gained more than anything else. They took him and plucked out, spear by spear, all the hair from his head, with the exception of a single lock on the top of the skull, called the tuft-lock, which was about three inches in diameter; then they put him through the process of having the white blood washed out of him; next he was carried to the Council House, where he listened to a set speech, setting forth the dignity of his new character, and the services expected of him as the son of a chief and the member of the tribe. Finally he submitted himself to be painted all about the face, in most fantastic devices, and then he sat down with the rest of them to a feast and to the pipe which is symbolic of peace and fraternity. Boone's best friend would not have been likely to recognize him, had he seen him thus metamorphosed.

Every day he studied how he might make his preparations most skillfully for escape. The Indians kept a close watch on him, though he believed they had confidence in his integrity. When they gave him bullets with which to go out on his hunting excursions, they were careful to count them, and observe on his return if he had secreted any for his own use in the future. But even here Boone was too shrewd for them; for he would use but slight charges of powder, and the bullets he would cut in two! Besides sending him out to hunt and bring in wild game for them, the savages set him at work making salt; this they knew he could do, for when he was surprised and captured by them, he was with a party that were engaged in this very occupation. There were salt springs on the Scioto River, and thither he was forced to go and manufacture this indispensable commodity for his dusky captors. The Indian was too proud to do menial work, and therefore left it for his squaws and his captives. Boone did not in any one point disappoint their expectations. He worked industriously and cheerfully; he produced liberal supplies of the article they wanted, and they bestowed on him their praise for his valuable services.

All this time, they were without their old leader at the fort at Boonesborough. More than four months had elapsed already, and nothing had been heard of him. It was most natural to conclude that he was dead, or had gone away into a captivity from which there was no hope of return. If they had been able to hear nothing of him, neither had he of them. He had undoubtedly received reports from Detroit, through the Indian runners that came in, from time to time, from that far-off locality, and those reports were anything but pleasant to his thoughts; for they told him of dark hours for the resisting colonies, sad reverses to their fortunes, and cloudiness for their prospects.

Presently, however, news arrived in a round about way at Boonesborough that their leader had been carried off to Detroit. That was all they could learn of his fate. They supposed now that he was altogether in the hands of the British, and that the Indians would have no more to do with him. And not having heard further respecting his disposal, the general conclusion was that he had been carried still further away into the wilds of Canada. Little thought they that, at that very hour, he was so near them, the adopted son of a powerful Shawanese Chief, and secretly plotting how he could best get back to them again! But, without Boone, they seemed to give up all; he had so long been their guiding spirit, animating them to exertion, that when he was lost, all seemed to be lost with him. Hence they fell off in their watchfulness against the enemy, and even suffered the fort itself — the last hope and stay of their existence — to be neglected. The strength of the fortification may be best understood from the following brief description: —

"It was a perfect parallelogram, including from

a half to a whole acre. A trench was then dug, four or five feet deep, and large and contiguous pickets planted in the trench, so as to form a compact wall from ten to twelve feet above the soil. The pickets were of hard and durable timber, about a foot in diameter. The soil about them was rammed hard. All the angles were small projecting squares of still stronger material, and planting, technically called *flankers*, with oblique port holes, so that the sentinel could rake the external front of the station, without being exposed to shot from without. Two immense folding gates were the means of communication from without."

Satisfied in her own mind that she should not hear from her husband again, the wife of Daniel Boone started off with her little family — excepting one daughter — for the home of her parents in North Carolina. She made the journey on horseback, carrying her few effects along with her the best way she could. It was a sorrowful journey indeed for her. Since coming out into the western country, she had sacrificed her eldest boy and lost her husband. Were there anything now left to stay for, she would willingly have remained on the frontier; but she despaired of ever seeing her husband again, and the condition of the settlers at Boonesborough was fast becoming so precarious that she could not but see the folly of staying only to throw her life away. Safely, though slowly, that brave woman, with her little brood about her, found her way back through the frowning wilderness, hundreds of miles, to Carolina. Few of her sex could be found willing to undertake such a journey even in these times; what is to be thought of the courage of her who freely set out on it, in times of peril like that, when the forest was alive with dangers from savage and beast, and not even a regular trail was to be followed from one point to another? Surely, that she was entirely worthy of her noble husband. She arrived home in safety, as every reader is glad to know.

To return to Boone himself. When he had finished making salt and gone back to the Indian settlement at Chillicothe, he was not a little surprised to find that his captors had been making preparations, in his absence, to proceed in full force against the fort at Boonesborough. There were four hundred and fifty of their bravest warriors, all ready to set out on the expedition. This fact caused him to hasten his plans. He began to hurry now, where he had acted leisurely before. But it would not answer for him to betray the least anxiety, or even suspicion; therefore he pretended not to notice that anything appeared different to him from what was usual.

In this way he could overhear the whole of their talk, and get at the meaning of their plans. They had no idea, either, that he had so good a knowledge of their language; but Daniel Boone was a man who put everything that came in his way to good use, at one time or another. He heard them talk of the weakness of the fort at that particular time; of the carelessness with which it was garrisoned; of the neglect into which it had fallen; and of their expectations to surprise and capture it beyond the possibility of a doubt. No one can imagine with what pangs his heart was visited, for he believed that at the fort were still his wife and children; still he was forced to appear perfectly calm, or all would be lost. It was a trial such as very few men could go through. Nay, more and harder than this; he had even to flatter and cajole the rascals whenever they did something which they deemed worthy of praise. Even upon the preparations that were making all around him for this very enterprise, he was forced to look with complacency and apparent satisfaction.

He knew he must escape, and that speedily. Yet

with the utmost caution. A single hasty movement, a single false step, however slight, would betray all. The 16th of June came. Up to that very day, the Indians had felt no suspicion of his intention. On that morning he was going out again, with their consent, to engage in hunting. He rose early, took his gun, secreted a small piece of venison to allay hunger, and started off. His heart swelled, courageous as it always was, to think of the great risk he was running. They would easily overtake him, if they should suspect for what he had gone forth; and once overtaken, his doom was sealed. They would never have permitted him to live to deceive them again. He was intensely excited, and yet he kept cool. To get a fair start was his great object. He knew quite as much of the wilderness as they, and would not be afraid to trust his own skill in woodcraft against theirs. He was in the prime of life, too, fresh and active; and he felt no fear, great as were the odds against him, unless it should come from some unforseen mischances.

For four days and nights he kept travelling. always in the direction of the fort, and, in the course of that time, he said that he ate but a single meal! The distance to Boonesborough was one hundred and sixty miles. This was at the rate of about forty miles a day. The single meal eaten by him on the road consisted of a wild turkey that he shot himself, after he had got safely across the Ohio River. When once he had passed this dividing line, he began to feel more at his ease, though still anxious, and all the time steadily pushing forward for the fort. It was his great care, too, to mislead his pursuers, or throw them off the trail; this cost him much trouble. He swam rivers, forded creeks, waded through swamps and marshes, and found his way through forests and almost impenetrable canebrakes. He listened to every sound, lest it might be a dusky pursuer. He was no swimmer, or at least a very indifferent one, and he doubted if he should be able to cross the Ohio safely, especially as its current was much swollen at that season of the year. But when he came to that great stream, flowing on so majestically, he had the luck to find a canoe that had drifted into the bushes on the bank near by, into which he jumped with no sort of ceremony; and he paddled himself to the opposite shore as fast as ever boat was propelled by oars before. It is said there was a hole in one end of the canoe, but that he managed to stop effectually, and in a very reasonable time. It was certainly providential that it happened to be hidden there in the bushes, and so he recognized the incident. When he reached the fort at last, and duly made himself known to his former comrades, they looked upon him as upon one risen from the dead. He was some time engaged in satisfying them of his identity, and afterwards in narrating his story from beginning to end.

It grieved him to learn that his wife and children had gone, but it was too late to help that. He set about directing the needed repairs for the fort. knowing far better than the garrison what were the preparations making, and what now were the many times heightened motives for investing and destroying it. All his energy was brought to bear upon this single thing. Where it was weak — at the gates, the flankers, the posterns, or the bastions — he made it strong again. He infused into them an activity and enthusiasm they had not displayed since the days when he used to arouse them to exertion before.

In the short space of ten days they were all right again, ready to receive any sort of a visit — outside, of course — which their old enemies might think best to make. This time he felt sure that the fort would be compelled to stand a siege it had never passed through before. He had seen with his own eyes the large preparations made by the Indians to invest and capture it. He had heard their talk about the matter with his own ears, and could not be deceived. Hence he well knew that when the next wave rolled in upon them, it would be the most terrible of any that had hitherto given them a shock. Against this he was bound to make all possible preparation. Besides suspecting what he did, he had, it seems, heard directly from the Indians at Chillicothe. One of his comrades had made his escape also, and came in with fresh reports of what the Indians were doing. They were all up in arms about his having left them in the style in which he did, and vowed vengeance on his devoted head for having so thoroughly deceived them. They held a great council forthwith. The matter was fully debated. It would not do to let a prisoner like that escape. They would teach him that the pride of the red man could not thus be offended with impunity. They, in their turn, too, were informed how the improvements in the fort went on. It was evident to them that the old hand of the master was there again. The intelligence of the strengthening of the white man's fortress excited them inexpressibly. They were impatient to be off, and make the assault they were resolved upon. They knew that every day's delay now only added to the white man's strength. The talk was long and earnest. It was obvious to them that they had no common enemy to deal with now, and they remembered that he was familiar with all their habits, their customs, and their weaknesses. He had shown the Indian, if no other white man had done it before him, that he was more than a match for him on his own ground, that he was acquainted with his tricks and traps, and knew how to keep himself out of them; and that the Indian, with all his boasted cunning, must needs be on the alert, or he would suddenly find himself outwitted by the very enemy he pretended to hold in such contempt and disdain.

CHAPTER X.

SIEGE OF BOONESBOROUGH.

THE Indians formed the grand plan of exterminating the whites altogether. They had witnessed their numerical growth since the day when Boone himself, the first settler, looked upon the unexplored solitudes. They remembered from how small a beginning this now formidable power had grown. If it was left to make its way unobstructed, there was no telling how soon it would be able to overwhelm them all. It was but natural that the red man should regard the enterprise of the white man with feelings of jealousy. There was a world of power wrapped up in the movements of the latter, whose sudden development might drive the former out of his native wilds altogether. Something mysterious was secreted in the very mode of his movements. This fort itself was a vast wonder. The courage of the white man was something unlooked for. But, above all, the savage could not measure the character, or fathom the motives, or comprehend the power of the acknowledged leader of the whites — Daniel Boone; he was the profoundest mystery of all.

Hence, with such impressions strongly working on their untutored minds, they almost instinctively came to the conclusion that, in order to conquer the whites, they must destroy them; if they would be rid of them, it must be, not by expelling them from the country, but by exterminating them; not so much as a relic of their former existence in the wilderness was to be left, to testify that they had lived or died there.

To accomplish a purpose so fell as this, required the active strength of the entire nation. They rallied far and near. All their braves, young and old, assembled in force, prepared to carry out the plan proposed. From this Indian village and that they came in, duly equipped for the bloody enterprise. The old Shawanese sachem — he who had adopted Boone as his own son — was at the head. His heart could never consent to forgive the deceit that had been practised upon it by his pale-faced son. If he could taste the sweetness of revenge now, he would feel in a degree compensated for what his pride had suffered. It did not take a long time, therefore, for the village at Chillicothe to fill up with recruits.

Boone was on the alert. He knew the character

of the foe, and the necessity of timely preparation against their approach. He had made the fort strong and whole again, and felt assured that it was capable of offering an irresistible defence against them. And thus prepared, he sallied out with a party of nineteen men, determined to oppose them even before they reached Boonesborough. He would fain surprise their scouting parties, and perhaps cut them off! It was a plan entirely characteristic of Boone, and worthy of his tried courage and boldness. Instead of waiting for them to come to him, he would go out to them. In this sally from the fort, he and his party traversed a distance of one hundred and sixty miles. They struck off for the Scioto River, near which they suddenly fell in with a party of thirty Indians, who were on their way down to join the main body of the enemy at Chillicothe. The place where they met was at an Indian village on a creek known as Paint Creek. A battle was at once fought between the two parties. Boone proved more than a match for the red-skins, whom he compelled to flee with the loss of one of their number killed, and two wounded. The fellows made rapid tracks for their friends at Chillicothe, bearing along with them the unwelcome tidings of the affray. Of course the Indian leaders there were astonished beyond measure to learn that their old enemy had shown boldness enough to come out from the fort and offer them battle. Nothing now was thought of but to go forth, and overtake and destroy him, and all his men.

But Boone was prepared for a movement like this. He had no idea of being caught away from home by the main body of the Indian forces. Having once tested the quality of his men in an open fight in the forest, he was quite satisfied to retire with them to the advantages of shelter again. They had tasted danger outside, and the Indians, too, had been taught a wholesome lesson; and that was all Boone wanted. It was something, at least, to show the savages that they need not consider themselves safe from assault in any place, or at any time. Having compelled them to abandon their little settlement at Paint Creek, and leave their baggage, together with several horses, behind them, he was for the time satisfied. He was absent but a single week on this warlike excursion, in which time he had struck terror into the very heart of the enemy.

As soon as he reached the entrenchments of the fort again, Boone put the entire garrison on the lookout for the foe; it was certain now that they would soon be there. He had gone out to challenge them, and it was estimating their courage and character wrongly to suppose that they would pass such a challenge by. Nor did he expect this to be any common assault, such as he was already familiar with; all their old tricks and surprises, their deceits and impositions, could not be expected to produce any present effect; hence he argued rightly when he concluded that the attack to come next would be entirely new in its mode and results. He was aware of the fact, too — and it was one not to be put out of sight in the calculation — that the Indians would not fight this time alone, but under white leaders, men skilled in a warfare of which the savages knew little or nothing. There were the British to aid and officer them; and there were certain of the French in Canada, too, whose inclinations were not at all towards the cause of the white settler on the frontier, especially as it tended to the spread of colonial power from the seaboard over the western wilderness.

The men at the fort waited and watched patiently. They were soon repaid, too, for their trouble. Before long, the wilderness was alive with Indians, all armed for the final struggle. They came prepared to blot the settlement at Boonesborough out of existence. Their faces were painted after the most hideous fashion, and their bodies were clad with the most unique and oddly-assorted apparel. They came and sat down before the fort in full strength. The forest resounded with their hideous yells and war-whoops. Stalwart forms appeared from the distant shadows, every one the impersonation of hatred and revenge. They scowled the defiance they might in vain have tried to speak. On the right hand and the left, and far away in the front. these native warriors threw out their terrible threats. Boone felt that hope had gone — except it came through exertion. It was idle to expect quarter from an enemy that had been so many times baffled. If they once effected an entrance within their fortified enclosure, there was end of all things earthly for them. It was truly a dismal contingency to contemplate, but it doubtless lent fresh courage to the settlers, for it was the terrible courage that is born of despair, that dies, but never surrenders.

The commander of this body of Indians was none other than Du Quesne himself, who gave a name to a fort which will ever go with our history, and with which that of Washington himself is associated. Blackfish, the Shawanese sachem, held command with, not under him. There were about four hundred and fifty Indians in the besieging force, and a dozen Canadians. It may appear strange that the

French colors were thus displayed in this memorable fight, but the British conquest of Canada was not yet practically felt among the Indians of the far West, and this expedition, moreover, was of a partizan, rather than a national, character. Canada was still, in fact, French, though ruled over by Great Britain; and hence, though we were at the time at war with England and at peace with France, the spectacle was exhibited on this occasion of a Frenchman leading on a party of Canadians and Indians to assail an American garrison. The lines, however, were more carefully drawn, not a long time afterwards. The French government never desired that the United States should undertake an invasion of Canada, preferring — so say the documents that relate to that period — that Canada and the provinces should remain for the present under the military deminion of England. It is argued, on behalf of so strange a position by France, that she wished first to aid in securing a separation of the colonies from the mother country, *after which* Canada and the provinces would of their own free will return to their loyalty to France again. No other explanation of so strange a circumstance seems possible; and even with that, all men are not at this day satisfied.

The little fort that was the object of all this

preparation, garrisoned but sixty-five men. So few against so many; seven outside, against one inside! What a forlorn hope indeed did they entertain! There were helpless women and children within the walls to protect, too. They all waited for the first movement to be made.

It was made; but very differently from the stereotyped Indian method. Instead of rushing at the gates with their hideous whoops and yells, a different course was pursued. The savages adopted the method of the white armies in cases of siege, and sat down and asked the garrison to surrender, sending a messenger to the fort with that modest request. Boone answered that he wanted two days in which to consider. It appears that, as soon as he knew of the straits to which he was likely to be reduced, he despatched a messenger to the East, describing his condition, and soliciting immediate aid. It was to Col. Arthur Campbell that he sent the request, and within the two days specified he would be likely to hear from him. It was simply to gain time therefore, that he put off an answer to the summons. If Campbell should happen to come forth from the forest unexpectedly to the Indians, then he could himself sally out and attack them from the front, while the force of Campbell would fall upon them from the rear; and between the two fires, their strength must melt away. Military men wonder at the motive that could have induced Du Quesne to consent to the terms tendered by the garrison; yet it is possible that he thought he might obtain by diplomacy what he was not so certain to secure by assault, and the glory would be greater. At any rate, he influenced Blackfish and his party to wait for the two days asked for by Boone, which was all that was wanted. Meantime, too, the garrison could complete the arrangements necessary for sustaining still more successfully the threatened siege.

Du Quesne certainly showed a humane spirit. He allowed the women and children, in the interval, to go out and get water from the spring, with which to help along existence during the trial that was before them. The cattle, too, were all got in through the posterns, — a very necessary assistance in carrying the garrison through the siege. But Boone himself was very careful to give the enemy no advantage; especially was he solicitous that they should not capture his own person, for then the whole object of the expedition would be over. Hence, while he freely exposed himself to their sight, he was careful to remain under protection of the fort. In his going out and coming in, he became quite familiar with the enemy, many of whom knew him well at the Chillicothe village and would have been glad enough to lay their hands on him now.

But the time grew short. The two days were nearly spent. No Col. Campbell yet, emerging with succor from the shadows of the forest. The answer was to be finally given. All the good that could be gained by the delay, had already been gained; the garrison had been supplied with beef and water to stand the test and trial of a long siege. He saw now that he must act; words were idle. So he collected his little handful of men around him, and asked them which they preferred — resistance or surrender. He knew for himself that surrender was certain death, and resistance, at the worst, could be no more; yet he deferred to the opinions of the others. They were all ready with their answer; they would resist till the last hour of their lives — they would *never* capitulate. Death itself was preferable to disgrace of that character.

Therefore they made ready to fight. They understood how much more numerous the enemy were than themselves, but they would fight, nevertheless. The commander of the besieging force demanded his answer. Boone stood boldly on the ramparts and gave it — "We will fight so long as a man lives to fight," said he. It was enough. The die was cast. From that moment their lives depended on a successful resistance. It was said that the bold and brave manner of Boone struck dismay into their hearts. At any rate, their leaders must have seen how foolish they were in permitting the garrison to provision themselves as thoroughly as they did. But the siege did not begin even then. Du Quesne was not willing to give up his arts of diplomacy, thinking he might yet win by mere words. So he returned a reply to Boone's answer, telling him that Gov. Hamilton, at Detroit, wished to make prisoners of the garrison, but not to destroy them, and he requested him to send out nine men from the fort to make a treaty, in which case the forces outside would be withdrawn, and all would go back home without any trouble. In his account of the affair, Boone says, "This sounded grateful to our ears, and we agreed to the proposal." He agreed to it because he knew that Hamilton felt friendly towards him, and he further knew that if they fell into the hands of the besiegers as regular prisoners, there was no hope for their lives.

On consultation, it was resolved to select the nine men desired and send them out. Boone, of course, was at their head. His brother was likewise of the party. The very best men of the garrison, in fact were the ones selected. Yet they determined not to go beyond the protection of the fort itself. The distance they ventured was one hundred and twenty feet from the walls. The accurate shooters of the garrison, with sure rifles at their shoulders, held their muzzles in such a position as to protect them. The leading men of the opposite party came up on the same ground. It was plain, however, that they took precaution to protect themselves as much as the others. There they met, professedly with only peaceful intentions, but in reality dreading each the power and threats of the other.

The Canadian captain proposed the terms. In order to test the sincerity of the besiegers, and for nothing more, Boone and his party consented to sign them outright, even though the conditions were such as they well knew they could not agree to Boone employed the occasion as a mere *ruse,* in order to find out their real meaning and intention. The treaty, therefore, was signed. Blackfish, the old Shawanese chief, then rose and commenced a speech. The Indians came forward at the same moment. He said it was customary, on the conclusion of a treaty of peace, for the parties to the treaty to come and shake hands with one another. Boone and his other eight men were alive to suspicion, but still they consented to go through with the ceremony. The moment hands were joined, a signal was given by Blackfish, by previous concert, and three Indians sprang forward to each white man, to make a captive. But, fortunately, the whites were fully prepared for them They broke away from the grasp of professed friendship, and ran for the fort. A general firing began. The party stationed at the fort let off their guns to protect their fleeing comrades, and the Indians commenced firing in return. Boone had thus unmasked their whole scheme, and had literally drawn their fire. Their entire plan was now exposed. The brother of Boone, Squire Boone, was wounded, but all the rest escaped as by a miracle. Nine men out of the jaws of four hundred and sixty! It was indeed a miracle.

Having secured their retreat within the fort, and closely shut and fastened the gates, they made instant readiness to sustain the worst that might come. And immediately, too, the siege began in good earnest. The Canadian and the Indian united their skill and perseverance. For nine days and nights this trial proceeded. It is impossible to convey to the reader any proper idea of what the garrison in that time went through. They were few in numbers, and their hopes were feeble. They were far from their friends, far from all succor and sympathy. The enemy could keep constant watch, and not suffer; but if the garrison watched, as they must, they were so few that all would be likely in the end to be exhausted. Every man, during that memorable siege of nine days, proved himself a hero. The great West knows not how much it owes to the exertions of these same brave pioneers, who were willing and ready to endure so much. The firing of bullets from the outside was incessant; it literally rained bullets, by the hour at a time, But the men in the fort were prudent, and used their ammunition only to the best advantage. They fired only when they were pretty sure to hit. The savages sheltered themselves as well as they could in the belt of the forest hard by, but even then the marksmen within the fort were much too sure for them. To show the amount of ammunition used by the foe, it is only necessary to note what Boone himself said about it, that "after they were gone, we picked up one hundred and twenty-five pounds of bullets, besides what stuck in the logs of our fort, which certainly is a great proof of their industry."

It is related, among the incidents of the siege, that a negro had deserted from the fort, who was known to be skilled in the use of the rifle. Anxious to commend himself to his newly-found friends, he climbed into a tree, and began to do serious execution. Boone heard what was going on, and looked out for the fellow. As soon as he saw his head, he fired a bullet into it, and the negro fell dead to the ground. Boone's daughter also was wounded — the only one who had remained behind when her mother set out on her return to Carolina. At length, exasperated to find that they could gain no advantage thus, the savages resolved to try another plan. They set fire to the fort! The flames were soon spreading! Whatever was done, must be done instantly. A young man was bold and brave enough to risk his life in the attempt to quench the flames. He succeeded in his effort. The fort was saved. Seeing this, the Indians thought they might as well give it all up. They took counsel among themselves forthwith, and resolved to withdraw without delay. There was no use in keeping up the attempt to subdue an enemy whom the Great Spirit had willed should *not* be subdued. But before they withdrew, they resorted to one expedient more. They attempted to undermine the fort. Boone, however, was on the alert, and foiled them with a counter-mine. They felt that they were vanquished, and gave it up.

The siege had lasted in all, from the 8th to the 20th day of August. It was a memorable affair in the history of the West, and cannot be dwelt on too long or too often by those who, in this day, enjoy the benefits that were secured to them by these bravest of all pioneers. Nothing more desperate in all history is recorded, when we take into account the circumstances of the time, and the several incidents of the occasion. To the last day of their lives, the men who participated in these stirring scenes were wont to recall them with expressions of the deepest emotion. They could never forget the fearful trials to which, in that brief time, they were subjected.

The savages went their own way. They hated to give over their darling design to make a captive of the man who was the acknowledged life and soul of the settlement, knowing very well the sort of man they had once had in their hands. But it seemed they were not fated to have him in their power very soon again. All their plans had certainly failed to retake him. They vanished as they had come, and the dusky retreats of the great forest received them.

Of killed, they lost thirty-seven, while the exact number of the wounded is not known. It is undeniable that upon the successful resistance of this little garrison, as upon a pivot, turned the entire fortunes of the British power at the West. Had they succeeded in overwhelming Boone and his garrison, there is no disputing that the colonies must have been pressed by the enemy, both in front and rear. But Providence ordered and arranged otherwise. "Man proposes, but God disposes;" — it was strikingly illustrated in the fortunes of the frontier settlers of the trying times of the Revolution.

CHAPTER XI.

MISFORTUNES AND TRIALS.

THE brief and modest statement of the Pioneer, after the siege of Boonesborough was raised, is as folllows: "Soon after this, I went into the settlement, and nothing worthy of place in this account passed in my affairs for some time." His successful holding out at the fort, however, was an act memorable enough of itself to answer for his lifetime; for, had this little frontier fortress gone, with the clouds of misfortune that were gathering over the American cause in the Atlantic States, there is no telling if it would have been possible to recover from the blow at all. More depended on this very defense of Boonesborough than the careless reader of our history is aware of.

He says of himself again: "Shortly after the troubles at Boonesborough, I went to my family, and lived peaceably there. The history of my going home (to North Carolina) and returning with my family, forms a series of difficulties, an account of which would swell a volume, and, being foreign to my purpose, I omit them."

Emigration westward soon began to set in. People, on seeing Boone safely returned home, had confidence to believe that the position of the settlers in Kentucky could be held against any odds. The trial to which they had been subjected already, went to prove that they could easily sustain even more.

The next year was 1779. The dark days of the Revolution had been thoroughly tried. There were a great many in Virginia and Carolina at that time, who wanted very much to exchange poor farms for rich ones, such as were described to them as abounding in Kentucky; and hence emigration commenced with a good deal of spirit and energy. Seeing the course matters were taking, the government of Virginia resolved to act for her own advantage without delay. A land office was forthwith opened. A regular board of adjudicators were selected from the most respectable citizens, who were to form a court, and go about from one place to another, where the land that was to be entered lay, and give and confirm titles. The names of the first Virginia Commissioners were, Edmund Lyne, William Fleming, Stephen Twigg, and James Barbour. They opened their office on the 13th of October, 1779, and Isaac Shelby, the first Governor of Kentucky after she became a State and was admitted into the Union, made the first entry of land therein, he having raised a crop of corn in the country in the year 1776.

The rage for the possession of land became almost furious. Speculators came forward, and vied with the hardy pioneer for the dominion that was to make them wealthy and powerful. The law read, " That any person might acquire title to so much waste and unappropriated land as he or she might desire to purchase, on paying the consideration of forty pounds for every hundred acres, and so in proportion." The Treasurer received the money, gave a receipt, and that receipt, on presentation to the auditor, entitled the holder to a certificate that he was possessed of so much land as was therein specified. There was much confusion and collision between those who held under the old Transylvania Company of Col. Henderson, and the present authorities of Virginia, and years passed away before the several points of law in dispute were finally settled.

Boone, like all the rest, was very anxious to secure for himself an ample estate in the country whose fertility he had first discovered. So he packed up his traps, and, taking counsel of his considerate wife, laid out what money he could collect together in land-warrants, and started for Richmond to prove and certify them in the proper court. The whole amount of money thus invested by him was twenty thousand dollars. This comprised nearly his all. On the way from Kentucky to Richmond he was cruelly robbed of the whole of them, and left almost destitute. Others in Kentucky had entrusted to his care their claims also, and these had gone with his own.

This was bad enough for any man. To add the last sting to his misfortunes, he was blamed by those whose property he had thus lost, and even charged by them, in some cases openly, with having kept their money for his own uses! There was a loss both of property and character. But these losses of the others he lived to return again. He was not the man to let such imputations against him sleep, without proving them false and impossible. Yet, so far as the Old Hunter was concerned, it was just as well as if he had not lost his own warrants; for had he located them, he would have been dispossessed afterwards by the technical constructions of the odious law itself, and he had better be robbed outright and all at once.

Now he saw, more than ever, the need there was of making exertions. He had a large family around him, and he was a poor man. He was in the prime of life, being only forty-five years old, and ready to do his part anywhere. Without delay he started straight for Boonesborough. His brave wife resolved to be his companion on the road. Readers in these days cannot appreciate the rare courage that was shown in this determination of the wife of the Pioneer. They cannot understand the nature either of the trials or the perils through which she was compelled to pass.

According to our hero's own account, he "settled his family in Boonesborough once more." Once within the walls of the fort, where he had been the author of such brave and noble deeds, the old memories revived within his manly breast. It is not to be questioned that all there felt the strength of a new courage when he came among them. Nor was he very much too early for the supply of the want that was to be made known. Gen. Clarke, of whom we have spoken before, had won some most brilliant victories over the combined forces of the British and Indians, taking prisoner even Governor Hamilton himself, who had command at Detroit when Boone was there a prisoner. In return for all these reverses, a large organization was set on foot for the reduction of Boonesborough, and the expectation was that it would be captured without much trouble. The whole united force of the expedition numbered about six hundred persons. They carried with them two pieces of cannon, and there was where they failed. The reader does not know the difficulty of taking cannon over smooth roads even; and when they have to be dragged through the woods by main force, as must have been the case in that expedition, it will be more readily understood why the whole plan was finally abandoned. It was fortunate indeed for the settlement that the enemy came to the determination, as they did, to give over their design.

About this time, too, Virginia recognized Boonesborough as a town, with all the dignity and rights of a township; and Daniel Boone was named as one of the trustees in the act of incorporation. It was publicly directed that every man who would erect a dwelling-house sixteen feet square, with a brick, dirt, or stone chimney, should receive a very liberal grant of land within the limits of the township.

Gov. Morehead, of Kentucky, in a public discourse on the history of this famous town, remarks: — "Time has passed roughly over the consecrated spot of the first settlement of Kentucky. The 'lots and streets' of Booonesborough have ceased to be known by their original lines and landmarks. The work of the pioneers has perished. Scarce a vestige remains of their rudely built cabins and their feeble palisades. The elm under whose shade they worshipped, and legislated, and took counsel of each other for safety and defence, no longer survives to spread its ample canopy over our heads. But the soil on which they stood is under our feet. The spring at which they slaked their burning thirst, at every pause in the conflict with the remorseless foe, is at our side. The river from whose cliffs the Indian levelled his rifle at the invaders of his hunting ground, still rolls its arrowy current at our backs. These are the memorials that cannot fail."

Boone had not been long at Boonesborough, before he projected an expedition to the Blue Licks, a place with which he was perfectly familiar. His brother Squire accompanied him. This was in October, 1780. It was the 7th day of the month when they set forth. Whether his object was to procure salt, or for some other purpose, does not appear; it may have been only from his love of adventure. They reached their destination without any trouble, accomplished the business on which they came, and set out on their return. As they started, a party of Indians who were secreted in the bushes, fired on them, and Squire Boone fell to the ground, mortally wounded. Daniel was obliged to flee, in order to save his own life. The savages scalped their dying victim, and put chase after the brother. But few Indians were a match for the great Pioneer in running, or in fighting. They followed him closely for a distance of three miles, and then gave him over. He was too shrewd and fleet of foot for them. It is related that a dog who had joined them in the pursuit, kept on after they fell back, and that Boone turned suddenly and shot the dog, and then pushed on again. He found his way back, sad and alone, to the settlement. Thus had Daniel Boone sacrificed both son and brother in his hard experiences on the frontier; a costly sacrifice indeed for the sake of those who were to come after him.

The following winter was one of the most severe ever known in the history of this country. Old men rehearsed the sufferings it entailed, when they forgot to talk even of the trials of the American army itself. Boone says of it, in his written account: "The severity of the winter caused great difficulties in Kentucky. The enemy had destroyed most of the corn, the summer before. This necessary article was scarce and dear, and the inhabitants lived chiefly on the flesh of buffalo. The circumstances of many were very lamentable; however, being a hardy race of people, and accustomed to difficulties and necessities, they were wonderfully supported through all their sufferings."

The American soldiers endured untold sufferings during that never-to-be-forgotten winter. All trials then seemed to come together. It was a sad winter indeed for Daniel Boone, for the blow struck at his heart by the violent death of his youngest and best beloved brother was one from which he could not all at once recover. Perhaps, at this particular period, cold and gloomy as it was, he suffered more than at any other time of his varied life.

The Land Commissioners having finished their business in Kentucky, a very large emigration set in, in the spring of the year, so that when the hard winter came on the sufferings were multiplied. It is said that the snow on the ground did not thaw, from the middle of November to the middle of February; and that fact supplies the staple of the entire story. Cattle perished all around the settlements. Wild beasts died without number, unable to resist the influences of the cold. Bears and buffalo, deer and wolves, and wild turkeys, were found everywhere, having yielded to the freezing cold. The old settlers never forgot the biting and bitter experiences of that season.

The number of settlers continued to increase in the following year. Boone stayed in Boonesborough still. In his narrative he says that an old Indian took him by the hand, one day, and said: "Brother, we have given you a fine land, but I believe you will have some trouble in settling it." He adds, very pathetically, — " My footsteps have often been marked with blood."

That year passed without the occurrence of any events worth rehearsing. The land about the locality was coming to be taken up rapidly, and settlements abounded on every hand. But early in the following year (1782), the Indians became more bold and reckless. They made an attack on a settlement not very far from Boonesborough, and carried off a prisoner. A Capt. Ashton went out, with a small party, in pursuit of them. He and eleven of his party were slain, leaving but thirteen men of the little company he commanded. The alliance between the British and Indians, likewise, made itself apparent now in new acts of cruelty, for which no writer, calling himself civilized, would think he could find a poor show of apology in these times of ours. A tory renegade named Girty, made himself notorious in these bloody forays upon the whites, and his memory is kept in perpetual hatred and scorn throughout the West. A Col. McKee also performed his part in the same abhorrent service. Men like these inflamed the passions of ignorant savages, and coldly looked on to see the deadly work they had themselves projected.

There were constant alarms around the settlements, all through these days. The savages grew bolder, approached nearer, and left darker tracks behind them. They thieved and destroyed wherever they went. Party after party of whites went out against them, and almost always came back without some of their valuable men.

Finally, there was a grand concert on the part of several Indian tribes — the Shawanese, Cherokees, Wyandots, Tawas, and Delawares — to make another general and overwhelming assault on the settlements. Old Blackfish was not with them, for he had already been slain. The Shawanese dwelt on the Great and Little Miami, in five Indian villages; the Cherokees on the Tennessee; the Wyandots on the Sandusky; the Tawas, eighteen miles up the Maumee; and the Delawares on the Muskingum River. It was the most formidable project yet undertaken.

All assembled at Chillicothe, an old rendezvous. The chiefs of the several tribes met in the long council room for consultation. They debated long upon their plans for the utter destruction of the pale-faces, whose evidences of power began to accumulate with such rapidity. This was their last and greatest effort against the increasing strength and numbers of the white settlers.

Not far from Boonesborough was a place known as Bryant's Station. Bryant had married Boone's sister, and was slain in an attack made by a party of Indians, some two years before. It was the 10th of August, when some five hundred Indians and Canadians fell upon this place, and assailed it with all possible fury. The fight was hot, and after a short time, the savages having lost many of their number, they retreated. There were four white men killed within the enclosure, and thirty Indians outside. The latter, after vainly trying to frighten the garrison with their idle threats, left in great haste and confusion.

The tidings spread. Boone and his comrades held a council of war, the moment he heard of what was going on. Cols. Todd, Boone Harlan, and Trigg led off soldiers to the rescue forthwith. A son of Boone went along with him named Israel, and also a brother. The men named above were the bravest of the brave; their names are held in honored remembrance throughout the length and breadth of Kentucky. In this council of war which was held, Boone urged that instant pursuit of the Indians be made. There was a divided state of sentiment on the subject among the leaders convened. A great deal has been said and written about the motive that actuated this one and that, in the council; and unworthy sentiments have been recklessly attributed to one and another by men who could have, apparently, no personal interest in misrepresenting the facts. While they were deliberating, however, whether to go on or wait for the coming up of a party under Col. Logan, one of the officers in the council, McGary, broke short all further hesitation by shrilly sounding the war-whoop, and declaring that all were cowards who would not follow him! He said he would take them to the Indians at once. The greater part were unable to resist the impulse of the moment, and started off headlong, arms in hand. Boone and Todd, however, remained behind. They felt that nothing but increased danger could come of such rashness.

Scouts were sent out, therefore, by Boone, who examined closely all the ravines near the Licking

River. They came back and said that all was clear, but still Boone was not satisfied. Yet he went forth after the rest, prepared to give the enemy fight wherever he might fall in with them. The line of battle was formed by the troops, in regular order. Col. Todd, who was commander-in-chief, led the centre; Col. Trigg commanded the right; and Boone, the left. The river bends at this point like a horse-shoe. Trigg led on his men unsuspectingly. Suddenly a fire from the long grass belched forth into their ranks, carrying confusion and dismay everywhere. They were caught in an ambuscade, and that was just what Boone tried to have them look out for; this was the penalty they paid for their rashness.

Next, the Indians on the right fired their volley, which proved to be deadly in the extreme. Trigg's men broke and ran, and Todd's received the fire. It carried havoc and death into the ranks. And now nearly five hundred armed men, all foes, rose upon the settlers' force, and completed their work of desolation. It appeared as if warriors started out of the very ground, so thickly did they spring up. The whites held their ground with wonderful courage, and returned the enemy's fire as fast as they could. Yet it was almost a carnage, on that bloody day.

Col. Todd was mortally wounded, but kept his horse, and gave his orders while the blood flowed freely from his wounds. For the space of fifteen minutes this sort of work was kept up, the savages at last bringing the tomahawk into play, as well as the rifle which they had just learned to use. All the way to the river, the ground was strewn with the wreck of that brave little army of settlers. Boone's own son, Israel, who had insisted on coming with him, was slain, and Boone found himself almost surrounded, when he attempted to make his retreat. He was determined to bring away with him his dying son, but the attempt nearly cost him his own life. To leave his child behind him, no matter what the cost of bringing him along, was the hardest thought for his fatherly heart. The dying looks of his offspring plead eloquently with his feelings. His resolution was on the instant taken.

Few men, even among pioneers and hunters, could have cut their way through such difficulties and dangers as Boone did. The savages seemed to start up out of the very grass, firing at him with every step he took. The ravine through which he dashed was full of them. There was still a ford for him to cross, which he succeeded in doing by swimming. The others were attacked in the middle of the river by the red-skinned villains, and bloody work was made in the encounter. They fought hand to hand in the water, and the red streaks showed what execution was done. It was an awful crisis for that body of brave troops. They seemed to have come out purposely for their own useless sacrifice. A single act of rashness had accomplished all this. Had they followed the counsels of Daniel Boone, this last and severest trial might have been avoided, and they might have caught the Indians in a trap, instead of being caught in theirs.

He was unwilling to leave the body of his boy behind him, and so he grasped it in his arms and bore it away with him in his headlong flight. But it was a great hindrance to his own safety. He could have got on much faster without such an encumbrance. Still, it was a hard matter indeed for him to think of running from that dearly loved child, and leaving him to the tender mercies of a horde of savages, to be scalped, and tomahawked, and cruelly disfigured. No; his strong affection asserted itself at the moment; he could not permit himself to hesitate, and he flew with the senseless form in his arms. The Indians were on this side and that. The farther he went, the more densely did they seem to spring up around him. When he had reached a particular point in the ravine, where the shadows slept invitingly for secresy, a tomahawk was brandished over his head, and the burly form of a giant savage arose to dispute the way with him. Boone saw that it was action or death, and that instantly. He dropped the body of his son, quickly raised his rifle to his shoulder, and shot the savage dead on the spot! The thought of the loss of this other child, maddened the lion-hearted man, and nothing was then beyond the range of his infuriated will.

This was the great battle of the Blue Licks. In this encounter there were slain sixty-seven of the American force, including Cols. Todd and Trigg themselves. Boone became, in the retreat, separated from the survivors of this massacre, but as he thoroughly knew all the ways of the wilderness, he was not long in finding his friends again. It was a sad topic of reflection for him, this battle of the Blue Licks. He sent in the official report of the same, being the surviving officer in command of the regiment, to Gov. Benjamin Harrison, of Virginia, the father of the late President Harrison, and one of the signers of the Declaration of Independence, from which we extract as follows: —

MISFORTUNES AND TRIALS. 209

The report to Governor Harrison is dated,—
"August 30th, 1782.

"On the 16th instant, a large number of Indians, with some white men, attacked one of our frontier stations, known by the name of Bryant's Station. The siege continued from about sunrise till about ten o'clock the next day, when they marched off. Notice being given to the neighboring stations, we immediately raised one hundred and eighty-one horsemen, commanded by Colonel John Todd, including some of the Lincoln County Militia, commanded by Colonel Trigg, and pursued them about forty miles.

"On the 19th instant, we discovered the enemy lying in wait for us. On this discovery, we formed one column with one single line, and marched up in their front, within about forty yards, before there was a gun fired.

From the manner in which we had formed, it fell to my lot to bring on the attack. This was done with a very heavy fire on both sides, and extended back of the line to Col. Trigg, where the enemy was so strong they rushed up and broke the right wing at the first fire. Thus the enemy got in our rear, with the loss of seventy-seven of our men, and twelve wounded. Afterwards we were reinforced by Col. Logan, which made our force four hundred and sixty men.

"We marched again to the battle-ground; but, finding the enemy had gone, we proceeded to bury the dead. We found forty-three on the ground, and many lay about which we could not stay to find, hungry and weary as we were, and somewhat dubious that the enemy might not have gone off quite. By the sign, we thought that the Indians had exceeded four hundred; while the whole of the militia of the county does not amount to more than one hundred and thirty. From these facts, your Excellency may form an idea of our situation. I know that your own circumstances are critical, but *are we* to be wholly forgotten? I hope not. I trust about five hundred men may be sent to our assistance immediately. ° ° ° ° I have encouraged the people in this county all I could; but I can no longer justify them or myself to risk our lives here under such extraordinary hazards. The inhabitants of this county are very much alarmed at the thoughts of the Indians bringing another campaign into our country this fall. If this should be the case, it would break up these settlements. I hope, therefore, your Excellency will take the matter into your consideration, and send us some relief as quick as possible.

"These are my sentiments, without consulting any person."

CHAPTER XII.

LAND AND LAND-OWNING.

THE disaster at the Blue Licks put fury into the hearts of all the white men round about. General Clarke had a large force under his command at the Falls of the Ohio, where the city of Louisville is located, which he held for the purpose of acting on the defensive, and restraining the Indian outlaws; but the moment the news of the battle of the Blue Licks reached him, he resolved to put forth his strongest exertions, and strike terror into the hearts of the foe wherever he could find them.

An expedition against the savages, therefore, was forthwith undertaken. The little army under Col. Clarke pushed on by forced marches in the direction of Chillicothe, and had come within two miles of the village before their approach was discovered. Had it not been for this unexpected occurrence, it is likely that the butchery of the Indians would have been immense. But being apprised of their danger, and knowing in what a large force the invading whites were approaching, and, above all, feeling the deep guilt on their own hands for which the latter were coming to be avenged, they stole off from their settlement as shadows go skulking farther and farther into the forest at the approach of the morning sun. In a few minutes, Chillicothe was a "deserted village" indeed. There was not a red-skin to be seen within its limits.

The infuriated white men came hurrying up, bent on destruction alone. They applied the axe and the torch to the lodges of their enemy, and ere long there was not one standing to tell the simple tale that an Indian village had ever existed there. All the other villages in the vicinity were destroyed also, root and branch. Utter desolation marked the course of the avenging white man. Boone himself stood once more on the spot where he had been held a captive, and the adopted son of an Indian sachem. How different must have been his feelings now!

The savages learned a valuable lesson from this visitation of the white settlers, for they found out that there was that in them which nothing could conquer or overcome; the more they were assailed, the stronger they rose to meet their assailants every time. This last blow, in particular, was the heaviest that had yet been dealt out upon the Indian power.

About this time too. came the termination of the

seven years' struggle between the Colonies and Great Britain. Every sign naturally promised peace. Emigration to the West now set in like the steady flow of a stream. Settlers came out into the vast tracts with their families, eager to create a new life and better fortunes for themselves, without the delays and perplexities incident to existence in the older States. The land of promise was rapidly filling up. Farms were taken on this side and that, and log cabins dotted the pleasant landscapes. The settler's axe was heard far and near. The danger from Indian invasion was not, to be sure, over yet, but the white man took courage in the midst of friends and coadjutors, and went forward with his designs with all possible energy. Boone could now look about him with feelings of lively joy and thankfulness. He was the first white man who had made known to the rest the existence of such vast treasures. He was, as it were, the Columbus of this splendid territory. Through toil and danger, by effort and by bloody sacrifices, he had made good his claim to the land whereon he, with the rest, had settled himself, and, if any living man was entitled to his reward, he was that very man.

He settled himself down quietly and peacefully on his tract in Fayette County, and devoted himself to agriculture. It was necessary, however, that he should still keep his unerring rifle within reach of his hand, and that he should not for a moment omit any of that prudence and caution on which alone depended his personal safety. His attention was, as an agriculturist, given to the raising of tobacco, among other things, though he never ceased to hunt as he had always done from his youth up, following the course of the wild animal with all the zest that was inborn with his simple nature. At no time did he think of hanging up his rifle over his hearth, with the intention of not taking it down again. It had been his tried and trusty friend. No companion, unless it were his faithful wife, had been truer to him than that. He might be a soldier; he might likewise be an agriculturist, tilling the land for others' uses; but he could not help being a *hunter*, while he lived among men. Though his fame was not thus acquired, still this pursuit was the single aim, and solace, and delight of his life.

While engaged in tilling the soil, in the peaceful possession of his farm, the following incident is narrated of the manner in which he succeeded in escaping from the clutches of four Indians, who had watched their opportunity to capture him, and who certainly believed that this time they had got him. The story was told at the wedding of his grand-daughter, not many months before he died.

His tobacco-patch was situated at some little distance from his cabin, and near by it he had erected a shed, or shelter, for curing the stalks. This operation consists in splitting the long tobacco-stalks, as soon as they are ripe enough, and stringing them along on poles, or sticks, some four feet in length. These sticks are then held up on stakes again, arranged in tiers, one above the other, till the roof of the shed is finally reached. Boone's shed was about twelve feet high, and there were three tiers of sticks, or poles. The lower tier was hung with tobacco, and had become pretty dry already. He had climbed up one day, therefore, to remove this tier to the upper part of the shed, in order to make room for more, when suddenly four stalwart savages entered the door, each with a gun in his hand, and accosted him.

"Ah, Boone!" said they, "Now we got you! You no get away more! We carry you off to Chillicothe this time! You no cheat us any more!"

Our hero looked down upon them, and in an instant comprehended his danger. He saw that they all had guns, and he had none himself. To oppose them openly would result in his swift destruction.

Therefore he had recourse to his old knowledge of the Indian character, and instantly resolved to try stratagem. He began by parleying with them.

"Ah," said he, in reply, "old friend, glad to see you!" and he begged them to be patient till he could come down. But first he must needs see to his tobacco. They showed considerable impatience at his delay, and began to be suspicious that he might be studying up some trick by which to deceive them and effect his escape. But he told them not to be in too great a hurry, that he would get through with his job soon, and begged them to watch him just as closely as they could. In doing this, of course he knew that their faces would be turned up toward him.

He was still making talk with them, they watching him the while, and he promising that they should have all his tobacco when it was cured, when, getting all the dried stalks and leaves directly over their faces, he suddenly turned them so as to fall exactly upon them. At the same moment he gathered his own arms full of the leaves, and jumped down upon them, completely filling their eyes and mouth with the fragments and dust, blinding them, and throwing them into convulsions of coughing. They fell to the ground, unable to see what was the matter, or whither their prisoner had gone. He ran for his cabin, where the means of defence were at hand, and the red-skinned rascals continued to wallow about on the ground for some minutes, unable to find their way out of the place. They called him loudly by name, and cursed him with all the phrases used for that purpose in their tongue.

With increased emigration into Kentucky, the farms presented a much better appearance, and the settlers' cabins wore a look of more cost and attention. The latter were always built of logs, and in a rough manner at best; but they served well as a protection against both an enemy and the weather. These houses, too, had the look peculiar to warlike times upon them. There were gates to them that might be shut, like those of a regularly built fort, when the foe was seen to approach, and they bade defiance alike to their strategy and assaults. Then there was space enough within the enclosure to retain cattle and horses, by whose help a siege of considerable length might be bravely sustained. But with the dawn of peace, these precautions were neglected, and finally soon fell into entire disuse. The log-house of the laborious farmer best told the story of the changed times.

Kentucky had her own courts now, too, Virginia

having granted that boon to her in the year 1782; so it was not necessary now for the settlers to make the long journey to Richmond in order to settle or substantiate a land-claim, or perform any other business of a legal character. These courts right at home were the greatest blessing, and helped wonderfully in giving strength to the fast growing State. The first court held in Kentucky was held in Harrodsburg, but its sessions were afterwards removed to Danville. The first Judges of the Kentucky district were John Floyd and Samuel Mc Dowell; names that stand among the highest in the Old Dominion to-day, and of which their inheritors have every reason to feel proud.

In the year 1784, matters had begun to assume in Kentucky a peaceful and settled aspect. The narrative of Boone, dictated by himself, comes to a close at this date. His narrative closes, very aptly, with a certain document in relation to the Indians, to which Boone calls particular attention. We copy it here. It represents to be the speech of a government agent, named Dalton, to the savages, and their reply. The reader will see that they give, as the reason of their alliance with the English, the poverty from which they suffered. They make a begging request, too, for *rum* at the agent's hands, which was, without doubt, given to them. This is the white man's speech:

"My Children: — What I have often told you is now come to pass. This day I received news from my Great Chief, at the Falls of the Ohio. Peace is made with the enemies of America. The white flesh — the Americans, French, Spanish, Dutch, and English — this day smoked out of the peace-pipe. The tomahawk is buried, and they are now friends. I am told the Shawanese, Delawares, Chickasaws, Cherokees, and all other red flesh, have taken the Long Knife by the hand. They have given up to them the prisoners that were in their nation.

"My Children on Wabash — Open your ears, and let what I tell you sink into your hearts. You know me. Near twenty years I have been among you. The Long Knife is my nation. I know their hearts; peace they carry in one hand, and war in the other. I leave you to yourselves to judge. Consider, and now accept the one or the other. We never beg peace of our enemies. If you love your women and children, receive the belt of wampum I present you. Return me my flesh you have in your villages, and the horses you stole from my people in Kentucky. Your corn-fields were never disturbed by the Long Knife. Your women and children lived quiet in their houses, while your warriors were killing and robbing my people. All this you know is the truth. This is the last time I shall speak to you. I have waited six months to hear you speak, and get my people from you. In ten nights I shall leave the Wabash, to see my Great Chief at the Falls of the Ohio, where he will be glad to hear from your own lips what you have to say.

"Here is tobacco I give you; smoke and consider what I have said. Then I delivered one belt of blue and white wampum, and said, Piankashaw, speak, speak to the Americans."

To which the Piankashaw chieftain made reply in the following strain and style:

"MY GREAT FATHER, THE LONG KNIFE: — You have been many years among us. You have suffered by us. We still hope you will have pity and compassion upon us, on our women and children. The day is clear. The sun shines on us, and the good news of peace appears in our faces. This day, my father, this is the day of joy to the Wabash Indians. With one tongue we now speak. We accept your peace-belt. We return God thanks. You are the man that delivered us what we long wished for — peace with the white flesh. My father, we have many times counselled before you knew us; and you know how some of us suffered before. We received the tomahawk from the English. Poverty forced us to it. We were attended by other nations. We are sorry for it. We this day collect the bones of our friends that long age were scattered upon the earth. We bury them in one grave. We thus plant the tree of peace, that God may spread branches, so that we can all be secured from bad weather. They smoke as brothers out of the peace-pipe we now present to you. Here, my father, is the pipe that gives us joy. Smoke out of it. Our warriors are glad you are the man we present it to. You see, father, we have buried the tomahawk — we now make a great chain of friendship, never to be broken. And now, as one people, smoke out of your pipe.

"My father, we know God was angry with us for stealing your horses, and disturbing your people. He has sent us so much snow and cold weather that God himself killed all your horses with our own. We are now a poor people. God, we hope, will help us; and our father, the Long Knife, have pity and compassion on our women and children. Your flesh, my father, is well that is among us; we shall collect them all together, when they come in from hunting. Don't be sorry, father, all the prisoners taken at Kentucky are alive and well. We love them, and so do our young women. Some of your people mend our guns, and others tell us they can make rum out of corn. Those are now the same as we. In one moon after this, we will go with them to their friends in Kentucky. Some of your people will now go with Castca, a chief of our nation, to see his great father, the Long Knife, at the Falls of the Ohio.

"My father, this being the day of joy to the Wabash Indians, *we beg a little drop of your milk,* to let our warriors see it came from your own breast. We were born and raised in the woods. We could never learn to make rum. God has made the white flesh masters of the world. They make everything, and we all love rum.

"Then they delivered three strings of blue and white wampum, and the coronet of peace."

It seemed, however, for years after peace with Great Britain was concluded, as if it were next to impossible to make the Indians quiet again. They had been stirred up by this late British alliance to do what otherwise they might not have thought of doing, and it was difficult for them to unlearn lessons that had been taught them so thoroughly. The Atlantic States were in the enjoyment of peace and concord, but Kentucky was still a land disputed between the settlers and the red men, and the latter had not yet made up their minds that it would be necessary for them to surrender their rights to it.

It was reported about among the different settlements, in fact, that the Indians meant to make at least one more rally for the destruction of the whites and the recovery of their former rule, and that, to this end, most extensive preparations were making among a number of the tribes for a final grand descent upon them. These rumors occasioned a great deal of anxiety on the part of the settlers, compelling them to make unusual efforts to provide for the threatened emergency. They held a large assembly of their leading men at Danville, and counselled of what was best to be done. It was a matter of some doubt with them how far they could properly proceed in the enrollment of troops, since they were but a dependent colony, and had no original authority to create armies; and this, among other questions, was, without doubt one of the first circumstances that led to the separation, seven years afterwards, of Kentucky from her parent State, Virginia. The disputes about titles to land, however, entered as deeply into the subject as anything else.

The rumored invasion by the Indian tribes never took place. They had probably not forgotten the devastation of their villages by the infuriated bands of white soldiers, and may have been deterred by such considerations from undertaking what they knew would result in a more terrible punishment than any with which they had yet been visited.

Then followed convention after convention on the part of the settlers, to take measures for securing independent authority to the newly settled country, and otherwise make themselves known and felt as an individual power. These assemblies were all held in Danville, and from their frequency through a long course of years gave a peculiar character to the place in which they were held. Daniel Boone, however, took no active part in them, so far as we are able to learn. He was no talking man, either. If the forest was to be explored, or a fort was to be built, or Indians were to be repelled in one of their crafty and murderous attacks, it was he who knew how to lead off in the business; but the work of talking he left to other tongues.

We cannot follow out the history of these numerous conventions, whose labors finally resulted in the total independence of Kentucky as a State; nor, indeed, is it at all necessary. It does not closely enough relate to the personal experiences of the subject of our sketch. Still, it would be doing him great injustice to leave a single reader to suppose that he ceased to take the deepest interest in the fortunes of the noble State whose foundations were laid by his own hand. He was not the person to be indifferent when all the work he had thus far done was trembling in the balance against the selfishness or assumed authority of other men.

These Kentucky conventions brought out before the country some of the best talent it has ever had the good fortune to impress into its service. There was John Marshall, for instance, afterwards Chief Justice of the Supreme Court of the United States, who was the Secretary of one of the earliest of these meetings. He had just commenced the practise of law, having completed his legal studies by the aid of fire-light, and being entirely destitute as yet of money or friends. Then there was Gen. Wilkinson, too, whose name is held in the highest regard by all true Kentuckians to this day, for his gallant services at all times on behalf of the State to which he had given his heart. The delegation that was sent to Richmond, to lay the case thus made up by the convention before the authorities of the Old Dominion, was remarkably able, and performed its errand with unswerving fidelity. In this important service, John Marshall played no unimportant part.

But the subject was meantime assuming a new shape before the United States Congress. After the passage of sundry resolutions, this way and that, on

the part of Virginia and the Federal Congress, and
after a great many conventions were held in Danville on the part of the persevering Kentuckians,
Kentucky was finally admitted into the Union as a
sovereign State, by Act of Congress specially passed
for that purpose, on the 4th day of February,
1791. It was a glorious triumph, though no more
than a deserved one, for the brave hunters and
pioneers who had taken their lives in their hands to
found a new State in the wilderness.

All this while, Boone was engaged in the quiet pursuit of his agricultural calling. He was essentially
a man of peace. He delighted not in wrangles,
discussions, or misunderstandings; and though he
never faltered when it was fit that he should throw
his influence on the side of the independence of the
land he loved, yet he preferred to be found *doing*,
rather than *talking*. He could hunt better than he
could play the delegate. He loved the land itself,
crowned with glory as it was, far better than to hear
dry discussions about titles to strips of it.

For some seven or eight years, therefore, he
remained in a state of semi-solitude, with his family
around him. The current of his life now flowed on
so evenly that it would be difficult to say what incidents ever occurred to make even a ripple in its sur-

face. He tilled his fields and was at peace. He made his rifle his chosen companion still, and lived over again in the surrounding forest the simplicity and the beauty of that early pioneer life when all Kentucky was an unbroken hunting range for his feet. His dog followed him still, faithful to the noble master it knew so thoroughly. His cabin held enough of the necessaries, and the comforts, too, of life, and there he taught himself how to be truly and solidly happy. He watched the course of the sun and the seasons. With the ways of the wild beasts he continued, as in other days, to be familiar. There was scarcely a path in the woods which his keen eye could not detect, whether worn by the savage, or the beast he loved to pursue. There was the same grandeur in nature for his eye, and all the old and lofty influences crowded in upon his childlike soul. No man, either, felt more deeply the sweet enjoyments of home, though that home was continually beset with fears and surrounded with living and lurking dangers.

But he was made to understand, in time, that settling up a new country is not civilizing it. The forming of a State Constitution did not go to make him any more secure in the possession of his lands. Where he once held without dispute — except, perhaps, from the Indian—he now held at the mercy of those whose paper claims and pretensions were the most offensive things imaginable. He felt, in other words, the approach of those influences peculiar to the civilized life we make a boast of; and he knew that he was less secure now in the enjoyment of his land and home than when he had none but the red man for his enemy. It is a damning commentary to make on the character of our modern life and habits; yet in Boone's case it was a perfectly true and proper one.

On a sudden, the general disputes about the titles to land now broke out. Of all the men living at that day in Kentucky, Boone thought himself the last one likely to be disturbed in the enjoyment of what he had. He had been unfortunate once, and lost all; but in the interval he thought he had made all up again. How was he doomed to the bitterest of disappointments! The title, however it might have been concocted, was put before the occupancy! The speculator could drive out the brave and self-sacrificing pioneer! The penniless adventurer, with scheming and heartless attorneys at his back, could eject the man who for years had periled all for the very land of which he was then possessed! And this the law permitted. There seemed to be no help for it. The authority of the original pioneer and discoverer was not accounted equal to that of the man who held cunningly drafted instruments in his hand, and could quote nice technicalities in his favor.

It was not a very long story, nor are the details at this day known; but it brings a blush of indignation to the cheek of every true man, to think that the cruel result came at last. Boone was turned out of his home, and his farm became the property of another! He who had found this beautiful country in order that others might enjoy it along with him, had now no place, save perhaps the forest itself, in which to lay his head!

It is too sorry a fact for the men of these times to dwell upon.

CHAPTER XIII.

A NEW HOME IN THE FAR WEST.

IN the year 1790, Boone made a visit to the place where he was born, in Pennsylvania. Of course his journey lay through the almost trackless woods, with scarce a sign of the white settler anywhere along his lonely route. It was a pious deed on his part, betokening the thoroughly true nature that slept beneath his rough exterior. His world had so far proved a hard world, filled as it had been with the most sober experiences; but he did not repine, nor grow misanthropic. When he began to see the necessity of removing again, he affectionately cast a lingering look back at the place of his birth, and determined to visit it once more while he had it in his power to do so. Perhaps, too, he thought there might be some chance for him, with his family, near the spot where he drew his first breath; the people might be more kindly disposed to him there, or he possibly had a secret and hitherto unexpressed desire to lay his bones at last where he was born.

At any rate, though we have no record of this

journey back to Pennsylvania, it is pleasant to know that his family friends and acquaintances received him with marked kindness and attention. His services as an explorer of the wilderness were by no means unknown to them there, for his fame had traversed all sections of the land, long ago. Pennsylvania had grown wealthy and powerful since the days when his father's family left its limits, making a slow procession southward into Carolina. Compared with the wild aspect of Kentucky, it presented the appearance of an old and perfect civilization. But his visit was a brief one. He felt other calls on his time and attention.

We cannot say how long afterwards it was, but it is certain that it was about this time (1790), when he made up his mind to leave Kentucky forever. He who had made the discovery of this noblest of States, was now compelled to exile himself because others wanted the land he certainly thought his own. It shows how indifferent the current generation is to its real benefactors. It is much too busy about its own selfish interests, to give its attention to the men who are above thrusting themselves into notice, and who do not perform great services with the hope of setting up some claim afterwards. They let him depart, nor felt a pang of remorse that he had silently turned his back upon them.

It would be a sad enough sketch, did we possess the skill to present it, the feelings of this self-denying and truly noble man, as he took his little family and started off for Virginia. He must have thought of the time when he came into these wilds, with his brother for his only company, and that brother now sleeping in death from a murderous attack by the savages. He could not but recall the winter he passed alone in the wilderness, with not so much as a dog or a horse for a companion, and without a particle of sugar or salt. He probably recollected the sad scene through which his wife was compelled to go when the little party of settlers was suddenly set upon by the savages in ambush, and his first-born son was cruelly slain. Nor was he forgetful, either, of the death of his last son, Israel, whose corpse he brought away from the scene of the Indian massacre at Blue Licks, lest it might be mutilated by his old foes, the red men. All these facts lay deeply imbedded in his memory; and at the time of his final departure from the midst of a selfish and ungrateful body of settlers, he must have felt them rise to the surface with unwonted influence and power.

He was a poor man. The world was all before him again. Driven from one spot, he might go to another. His faithful and devoted wife was still faithful and devoted, even if all the rest of the world forgot him. She was willing to walk by his side wherever he went. And they went slowly and sadly out of Kentucky together.

It must have started tears in his eyes, when he looked for the last time on the fort his hands had assisted to erect in Boonesborough. Every rood of ground there was vocal to his heart. He had trodden every foot, and defended it with his own blood. Yet there was not room for him there any longer. The very Indians he had assisted to expel, were hardly more exiles than himself, or more gratefully thought of by those who remained behind. Twenty years before he might call himself — more truly than any of those who came after him — the owner of the whole of this noble tract of land; now he was driven forth from its limits, unable to find an acre that he might *legally* style his own.

The tract of land on which he had made arrangements to settle in Virginia, lay on the Kenhawa River. It was not like the land he had owned in and near Boonesborough; yet it was, to all intents and purposes, his own. There was not that margin in his new home for farming operations which he enjoyed in Kentucky, nor did he appear particularly sorry that it was so. He had had enough of semi-civilized life; now he meant to return to hunting and the solitudes again. And in this Virginia abode he was undisturbed in the enjoyment of his native propensity. The old delights of woodcraft he renewed in all their freshness. He was familiar once more with the fox and the red deer, the wolf and the bear. The winds fanned his weather-worn face, and brought back to his heart the old dreams of liberty and peace. In the silence of the forest he felt his soul grow calm again. The sense of hardship and wrong that had recently ruffled it, disturbing the even flow of his happiness, would all be sunk in the depths of the stream that once more flowed on as placidly as ever. This solitary hunter-life was Boone's true life. He was of that rare class of souls, like Audubon's, which live the most profoundly when closest to nature, and in whose ears the sound of human disputes are but precursors of the death of all further enjoyment.

His gun was at this time his constant companion. Its sharp ring awakened the wild echoes, far and near, and seemed to bring them around him like spirits, questioning him of his business and his name. Mr. Peck, who wrote a fine sketch of his life, says of the habits of the Hunter, which will apply to the same period of which we are now writing: "I have often seen him get up early in the morning at this season, walk hastily out, and look anxiously to the woods, and snuff the autumnal winds with the highest rapture; then return into the house, and cast a quick and attentive look at the rifle, which was always suspended to a joist by a couple of buck horns, or little forks. The hunting dog, understanding the intentions of his master, would wag his tail, and, by every blandishment in his power, express his readiness to accompany him to the woods. A day was soon appointed for the march of the cavalcade to the camping place. Two or three horses, furnished with pack-saddles, were laden with flour, Indian meal, blankets, and every thing requisite for the use of the hunter."

In the Kenhawa country, the life of Boone was not altogether free from the interference of the Indians, as it had been before. He was still obliged to guard against their craft and their treachery; if they could take him at an advantage, they certainly would. It was rumored in Philadelphia, in the year 1793, that the Indians had made an irruption into that country, captured Daniel Boone, and carried him away, no one knew whither. But such was not to be his fate. It is quite likely that he would never have been heard of again by civilized persons, had they once succeeded in carrying him off. But that they were not yet able to do. He was ever wary and watchful, knowing his danger. His long acquaintance with the habits of Indians, proved ample protection for him, when others would most likely have fallen a sacrifice to the superior sagacity and craft of his red-skinned foe.

It was while living thus alone and forgotten in the wilds of Virginia, that news came to Boone of a beautiful tract of country in the far northwest, then known as Upper Louisiana. It belonged at that time to Spain. From time to time, one and another came along with fresh intelligence of this great land, picturing it as surpassing in beauty anything they had ever rested their eyes on. Their stories fired the heart of the old Hunter anew. His imagination became inflamed again. His eye kindled, and he almost felt that the whole map of the country unrolled itself even then before him.

And there was another argument, and for his mind a very strong one — they told him of the simple state of the Spanish laws on the subject of land. He had had truly bitter experiences in connection with this matter, and whatever reminded him again of a country where the intricate and artfully-framed statutes in reference to the ownership of land, would be very likely to attract him beyond the power of his will to resist. He heard all the stories of the new land with delight. He sat alone and pondered these things. Having ruptured those ties of affection that held him to Kentucky, he cared not now whether he remained long in any one place or not; henceforth he was a citizen of the world, and could make his home as readily in one place as another. It was true, he would become the subject of a foreign power by emigrating to Upper Louisiana; but, as he said himself about it, " it was the country, not the government, of which he was in pursuit."

He was not long in making up his mind to leave the place where he was, and go out westward again. He would cross the flood of the Great Father of Waters, and be forever beyond the reach of those whose fraud and trickery had beggared him. The very resolution seemed to give him freedom again.

It has always been said of his free movements, that he went farther away from neighbors because he disliked the society of man; but, however just the remark might be, considering the manner in which his own race had treated him, there is no reason to believe it true. Daniel Boone was not a misanthrope by nature. No man loved home and family with a tenderer devotion. He had an undying love for the solitudes and secresies of nature, it is true; but that could never have soured his heart to the blessed influences of home and friends, or shut out from it the sweet solaces their presence always brings. We find no proof, in any record that is to be seen, of the charge that has been so often brought against him; on the contrary, we do know that he indulged in no idle or malicious complaining on account of his loss of money and lands, but, when he was cruelly robbed of all he had, he went quietly off into the wilderness again, determined to find peace, if he could not hold his home. There is every proof peaced, that Boone's nature was sweet and whole, and that he lost none of his happiness by indulging in feelings akin either to malice or envy.

The day came for him to start. It was the year 1795. The Hunter was now sixty years old. It was rather late in life for him to make another remove, but his heart was as young as ever, and his limbs were vigorous and active. He saw the world with a keen and bright eye, and guided his rifle with a hand that did not tremble in the least. In the refinements of civilization, men would be called *old* at the age of sixty, and very few would be thought able to make even temporary journeys, over smooth roads, to stay among relatives and friends; but Boone was so truly a child of nature that he was ready at any moment to accept all her hints, and could as easily remove his residence a thousand miles then as thirty years earlier.

It is to be considered, too, that he already had a son and son-in-law in Upper Louisiana, so that he was only going among friends again. The inducements which were held out to him besides, were many and tempting. His fame had preceded him there. He was known not only as a successful pioneer, but as a famous fighter of the Indians. The Spanish authorities wanted to secure the accession of as many men of his stamp as they could. It was plain to his mind, also, that the great northwest was the field for all exciting adventure in the future. There the world lay open for him; in every other direction it seemed to be closed.

Nor did he expect that he was always to remain a citizen of another country, for his eye took in the greatness to which the United States were already destined; in truth, he was one of the most marked Manifest Destiny men of his generation. In the course of his narrative, written down by Filson, and reviewed by himself, he says emphatically:

"I grant it will be absurd to expect a free navigation of the Mississippi, whilst the Spaniards are in possession of New Orleans. To suppose it, is an idea calculated to impose only upon the weak. They may perhaps trade with us upon their own terms while they think it consistent with their interest, but no friendship in trade exists when interest expires; therefore, when the western country becomes populous and ripe for trade, sound policy tells us the Floridas must be ours, too. According to the articles of the Definitive Treaty, we are to have a free and unmolested navigation of the Mississippi: but experience teaches mankind that treaties are not always to be depended upon, the most solemn being broken. Hence, we learn that no one such put much faith in any State; and the trade and commerce of the Mississippi River cannot be so well secured in any other possession as our own."

This was written eleven years before Boone made his removal to the very country of which he spoke.

This was the fourth time he had packed together his family goods and gone off into a new land. Born in Pennsylvania, he went first to North Carolina thence to Kentucky, next to Virginia, temporarily, and now to Upper Louisiana, for the remainder of his life.

This journey was a long and weary one. It was not made by rail, or even by stage-coach; nor were there canals stretching their sleepy lengths across the vast western States, connecting river with river, but his track lay along the line of the settlements, which were few and far between, until he reached the Mississippi River. The mode of conveyance was of course on horseback, for there were no roads in those days for wagons. The reader will therefore appreciate the rare courage, as well as the resolute endurance, by whose aid his true wife was enabled to accompany him to his journey's end.

The head-quarters of Spanish rule were then at New Orleans. Charles the Fourth was the monarch on the Spanish throne, but it is not likely that he had heard of this man whose rifle had thus opened the way for a nation. Yet his head officer at New Orleans had; and it is gratifying to all Americans at this day to know that Delorne, the Lieutenant Governor, offered our hero a welcome to the new territory every way befitting his name and fame. It was for the Spanish Governor's interest, it is true, to get such a man into the territory he held in the name of his royal master; for the Indians were exceedingly troublesome, and he was anxious to augment the strength of the settlements as fast as he could.

Boone, then, reached St. Louis; a flourishing trading post at that day, but giving no promise then of the grandeur of its present position, or its future destiny. He was welcomed by his son, Daniel M., and immediately he looked around and selected a place for his residence in the Femme Osage district. Of this district the Spanish authorities constituted him the Commander. He was thus made both a military and civil officer. The date of his commission was July 11th, 1800 — some years after coming into the country, and after thousands had flocked in to people a land that proffered such indescribable attractions. Those who came, too, knew the character of Daniel Boone full well.

As an act of gratitude to the great Pioneer of Kentucky for lending his influence in attracting such an emigration to the regions of Upper Louisiana, Delorne marked out a tract of land consisting of *eight thousand five hundred acres* for him, and made him a present of it; this land lay on the north side of the Missouri River. Now it seemed as if his wrongs were all set right once more; the cheating from which he had suffered in the matter of his Kentucky claims was generally recompensed here in these rich lands on the Missouri. But there was a fatality attending all his transactions, so far as their pecuniary value was concerned. It was necessary for him to go down to New Orleans and there complete his title, after the regular forms of Spanish law; but this was too much trouble for Boone, and he omitted it altogether. So that when the whole of the immense country known then by the name of Louisiana came into the possession of the United States — as he certainly foresaw it would, in time — he found himself again divested of a title to his lands, but this time by his own fault alone. He had doubtless counted on his title's being all the safer when the territory became the property of the government of his native country; but past experience should have taught him a lesson, which it seems it did not. And if he was careless of these matters himself, his friends should have taken them in hand on his behalf. Yet it is to be remembered that it was a very long journey to New Orleans from St. Louis, in those days, and that the Mississippi was not traversed with palaces of steamers as now. Boone was not thirty years old, either; he was sixty, and there was a difference.

Life was simple and peaceful all around him, while he held the office to which he was appointed.

No law-suits interfered with friendships, but whatever cases were brought to the attention of the Pioneer he was able readily to adjudicate. There were no thefts and no robberies. Men dwelt together after the primitive modes. There was no war, nor rumor of war. The atmosphere was that of peace. For these five years of his life, at least, he had known what it is to be undisturbed and happy.

Louisiana passed into the possession of France, in the year 1800. Napoleon the First knew what an immense tract it comprised, but he also knew that the glory of the Empire lay not in the New World. He conceived the grand design of making it over into the hands of the United States, and it became ours by regular purchase in 1803. This purchase was one of the most magnificent events in the administration of Jefferson, or, indeed, in the history of the country. Napoleon had a deep laid design in this transaction, too; he wished to augment the power of the young Republic of the West, that she might the sooner rival the pretensions, as she does to-day, of the great nation from which she had not long before made herself free. So that Boone became a citizen again of his native country, having thus belonged in his life to four different nations — Great Britain, Spain, France, and the United States.

For a long time he occupied himself with the hunt. After the upper country became ours, he went to live with his son, and busied himself almost all the time in that way. He had no great success at first, but he did not despair. After years of resolute endeavor, he succeeded in collecting peltry enough to bring him in what money he wanted, and, taking his hardly-acquired wealth about his person, he started off for Kentucky to pay his debts! He had left certain obligations behind him there. When his own land claims were in dispute, he was obliged to hire lawyers, as well as borrow from friends; there were also debts of honor resting upon him, such as those included in the amounts entrusted to him by neighbors and acquaintances, when he went from Kentucky to Richmond to buy lands for them and was robbed by the way. All these debts he determined to pay; and he paid them. He hunted up every man to whom he owed a dollar, asked him how much he owed him, took his own word only for the amount, and discharged the obligation. He kept no particular account himself, and he was willing to trust to the honesty of others. It was, unfortunately, owing to this very same spirit of his that he lost his claims to his own possessions.

Kentucky was greatly changed in his eyes, since

he saw it last. He could scarcely realize that there he was the original discoverer, and that the feet of white men never trod its virgin soil before his own. It seemed like a dream to him now, to think that his own wife and daughters were the first white women who stood on the banks of the beautiful Kentucky River, and that so little while ago! But silently and unheralded he came back into the State, to discharge a sacred duty; and in the same way he went out of it again.

Returning to Missouri, he employed himself with his life-long pastime of hunting. That was a second nature to him. He came back after paying his debts, with but half a dollar about him; but he felt rich in the consciousness of having fully discharged his duty. He owed no man anything. Could all say the same by him?

He was now hard upon seventy. Age began to make its slow but sure impress upon him. Yet he sallied forth without company, self-reliant and strong as ever. He skimmed the Missouri in his light canoe, and followed the beaver to their most secret domains. He camped out in the forest as he always had done, trusting to his rifle and his sagacity still. Sometimes he fell in with the Indian, but he knew how to evade his treacherous grasp. He studied the same arts by which to protect himself now, that he ever did. If he was surprised, he could offer as tough a resistance as the savage, single-handed, would care to cope with himself.

There is something not merely poetic and picturesque, but noble and grand, in the contemplation of the way of life followed by such a man, with such a weight of years upon him. It was a truly fit close to such a career. His rifle was his earliest friend, and it remained his latest. The woods drew him forth from home when he was a young man, and they offered him ten thousand sweet consolations, now that he was old, and those whom he had benefitted had forgotten him. If he was unquiet among men, nature ever offered him dreams of repose and peace. When he felt inclined to repine at the hardness of fortune, it was all forgotten as he lay his silvered head, like the mere child he still was, in the lap of the mother of us all.

CHAPTER XIV.

LAST DAYS OF THE HUNTEP.

IN pursuing his hunting, in these days, Boone traversed a wide extent of territory. He went as far even as the mouth of the Kansas River — a far off country then, but brought very near to us by the events of these later times. At the time he strolled off to this distance, a characteristic incident occurred, which ought not to be left out of any biography of such a man. We prefer to give it as we find it in the faithful sketch written by Peck, in Sparks' Series. He says:

"He took pack-horses, and went to the country on the Osage River, taking for a camp-keeper, a negro boy, about twelve or fourteen years of age. Soon after preparing his camp and laying in his supplies for the winter, he was taken sick, and lay a long time in camp. The horses were hobbled out on the range. After a period of stormy weather, there came a pleasant and delightful day, and Boone felt able to walk out. With his staff (for he was quite feeble), he took the boy to the summit of a small eminence, and marked out the ground in shape and size of a grave, and then gave the following directions. He instructed the boy, in case of his death, to wash and lay his body straight, wrapped up in one of the cleanest blankets. He was then to construct a kind of shovel, and with that instrument, and the hatchet, to dig a grave exactly as he had marked it out. He was then to drag the body to the place, and put it in the grave, which he was directed to cover up, putting posts at the head and foot. Poles were to be placed around and above the surface; the trees to be marked, so that it could be easily found by his friends; the horses were to be caught, the blankets and skins gathered up; with some special instructions about the old rifle, and various messages to his family. All these directions were given, as the boy afterwards declared, with entire calmness, and as if he was giving instructions about ordinary business. He soon recovered, broke up his camp, and returned homeward, without the usual signs of a winter's hunt."

The decision was rendered in the United States Courts, in the winter of 1810, that Boone's title to the great grant of land by the Spanish Governor, was not a good one, and he learned once again in his life that he was beggared. It was a hard blow for the old Hunter, especially at his time of life He had now reached his seventy-fifth year.

This was the time, if ever, it appeared to him, when he might with justice address a word to Kentucky. He sent a memorial to her Legislature, therefore, asking that body to see that some sort of justice be done him by Congress. The Legislature listened, and caused his petition to be heard properly on the floor of the United States Senate. The language of the preamble of the Kentucky resolution was this:

"The Legislature of Kentucky, taking into view the many eminent services rendered by Col. Boone in exploring and settling the western country, from which great advantages have resulted, not only to this State but to his country in general, and that, from circumstances over which he had no control, he is now reduced to poverty — not having, so far appears, an acre of land out of the vast territory he has been a great instrument in peopling — believing, also, that it is as unjust as it is impolitic that useful enterprise and eminent services should go unrewarded by a government where merit confers the only distinction, and having sufficient reason to believe that a grant of ten thousand acres of land, which he claims in Upper Louisiana, would have been confirmed by the Spanish Government, had not said territory passed by cession into the hands of the General Government, — *Therefore*, Resolved," etc.

It was eminently proper that he should petition Kentucky to aid him in memorializing Congress on his behalf, and it must have been an act of genuine satisfaction to the members of her Legislature that they had it in their power to serve the cause of the noble old Pioneer.

His request, owing to the influence of Kentucky in the national councils, was listened to with profound respect, and a grant was made to him of the public lands; but not to the extent to which the Spanish Governor had rewarded him. He would have been glad to obtain, on account of his children at least, the original number of acres bestowed by Spain; but the eight thousand five hundred were whittled down to eight hundred and fifty! Congress acts in just this unaccountable way. It rewarded Lafayette for his services in the Revolution, munificently — which every man is glad of; but certainly Daniel Boone had performed service second to that of no living man on behalf of the nation that had now sprung into the strength of a young giant among the older nations of the earth.

It is not the policy of our government, we well know, to openly reward men for patriotic services; yet there are petty partizans enough in politics, who go out of office rich in the goods of this world, while the solid benefactors, the brave Revolutionary soldiers, and the very founders of the nation, have died in poverty and want, and some with scarce a place to lay their heads.

The request of the Pioneer was granted, in the form we have stated, in the month of December, 1813; but she who had devoted a long life to his varying fortunes, had reared him children, had shared his trials, and solaced him in the midst of his troubles, she — the devoted wife and tender mother — had just passed away! She died in the month of March previous, at the good old age of seventy-six. Her eyes were closed, not amid the scenes of her childhood and youth, but far away in a strange land, with few ties to bind her to earth, and her spirit waiting and ready to be loosed. Her husband himself selected the spot for her burial. It was on the top of a ridge, which commanded a view of the Missouri River, and a place of surpassing beauty. There all was peace. He showed his friends in what way he desired to be buried beside her, and left her remains to their long repose. As we before remarked,

Boone was in his seventy-ninth year when he became the recipient of the land given him by Congress; and so near four-score as that, generally is out of the reach of wordly interests. The eye had begun to grow dim, and the hand to be feeble. Still all the native vigor and freshness of the noble spirit was left. It was not much that his country did for him at so advanced an age, but he said that what he got would be something to leave to those whom he loved. He wandered out still to indulge in his favorite pursuit of hunting, carrying his trusty rifle feebly, and being careful not to venture far away from home. The days glided by pleasantly for him, and the seasons rolled over his head with all their wonted delights. He rejoiced as keenly in the exhilaration of the open air as ever, preferring the free range of the forest and the prairie to the close quarters of the cabin fireside.

Indeed, there is no telling either the nature or the depth of the secret enjoyment that was his, in this placid evening of his life. Reflection was busy within him. Memory brushed up all the olden pictures of forest and river, of the hunt and the Indian warfare, and created the past newly for him again. If ever man had enough in his thoughts to keep those thoughts busily employed, **Boone was that man.**

His life was full of adventure and incident. His days were alive and swarming with fresh-coming experiences. He could plunge into the past at any moment, and find that he had entered a new realm. While he sat on the fallen trees of the forest, and suffered memory to run back with loosened rein, there was no need that he should make any drafts on the present in order to fill his heart with satisfaction and contentment. And in such a state of mind, he passed these slow-moving days.

Later than this, he removed to the house of his son-in-law, Callaway. He had married his daughter Jemima — one of the three girls who were run away with by the Indians from Boonesborough, and afterwards rescued by her father. With Mr. Callaway's family he lived the remainder of his days. It could not be said of him, however, as of so many men who pass on from four-score to ninety years, that he was troublesome or querulous; on the contrary, he was cheerful and contented to the last. It was while in this family that Mr. Peck saw him, in the course of the year 1818.

He describes him as having the appearance of a highly respectable old man, clad in homespun, neat in his attire and habits, in a little room of his own, which he kept in perfect order, with a clear eye and a very fair and pleasant countenance, a high and bold forehead, a marked nose, expressing decisiveness of character, and the sleek and silvered hair one would expect to find on a head so ripe in years as his. He was not, then, a rough or brutal man in his aspect, but wore all the evidences of refinement and real dignity. He carved powder-horns, by way of amusement, and toyed with his faithful old rifle as if it were a child; and in truth, it had kept him long and pleasant company. Even then — which was two years before his death — he was in the habit of strolling off, though not unattended, to indulge in a little hunting, eager to keep up the sport of his boyhood to the last of his happy days.

For several years he had kept his coffin constantly under the bunk in which he slept, and used to sit and regard it with a melancholy satisfaction. He thought of the chosen companion who had gone before him, and of the bliss of the coveted reunion. And he felt already at rest, in knowing where his body was going to lie when it had finished its earthly service. That ridge overlooking the Missouri was never out of his mind. She whom he loved was sleeping there now. The winds of heaven would visit them freely in that resting-place, and the people of a vast continent would come to see where the Pioneer and his faithful wife lay.

All sorts of stories were told of him while these last days wore on; and, now and then, he would hear of some of them himself. One was to this effect: it was reported that, while standing at a salt lick and watching for the approach of deer, he had raised his rifle to his shoulder to take a sight at one as he came down towards him; the old man died in the excitement of the moment, and was found with the rifle still at his shoulder, in the very act of taking aim! This story got into the newspapers, and finally reached his own ears. He smiled pleasantly when he heard of it, and only answered,—" I never would believe that, if I told it myself. My eyesight is too poor to hunt."

Stories of his misanthrophy were just as reliable as this; likewise those of his moving further away into the wilderness, when he found neighbors crowding up, and giving as the reason that he was too much crowded. All such tales were the mere imaginings of those who had been taught to regard the name itself of Daniel Boone almost as a myth, and had no foundation in fact whatever.

The famous American portrait painter, Mr. Chester Harding, paid him a visit in the last year of his life. This was in 1820 — a memorable year otherwise in the history of the Union. Mr. Harding found him, when he first entered his apartment, reclining in his bunk and roasting a piece of venison, which he was holding out on the end of a ramrod to the blaze of the fire opposite! It was an occupation quite befitting his age and character.

The old Hunter walked out with Mr. Harding every day while he remained there, and appeared as cheerful as usual. His recollection of recent occurrences was not at all ready, or accurate; but he would talk of what happened twenty, thirty, forty, and fifty years ago with all the warmth and eagerness of a boy. His heart was all in the past. There was nothing in that which he had forgotten. He never tired of telling over and over his old experiences with the Indians, or the tales of his skirmishes with the wild beasts of the forest.

It was while engaged in this sort of pastime, that Mr. Harding was able to catch that true expression of his spirit which he has fortunately handed down to future generations. This, we believe, was the only portrait of the man ever painted. It now adorns one of the legislative halls of Kentucky.

Just after the picture was completed, the old man was taken ill, but his constitution was too good to yield to the first assault of any sickness. He afterwards, however, made a little visit to the family of his son, and, while there, was taken down again, and yielded up his life. He breathed his last on the 26th of September, 1820, having reached the ripe old age of eighty-six. His end was peaceful and calm. His simple soul took its flight serenely, trusting in that God who had tenderly watched over him from the beginning. It was well that he who had gone through such varied scenes — of strife, and toil, and trial — should fall asleep at last in the bosom of his family.

His body was buried, according to his own request, by the side of her who had been faithful to him through life, on the ridge overlooking the beautiful river, the spot his own eyes had selected.

In this solitude, the Pioneer and his wife lay side by side for twenty-five years. The world in that time came and crowded thickly around them. Steamers ploughed the river, freighted with the wealth of a young nation. The sights and sounds of a new life began to abound on every side.

At the expiration of this time, the Legislature of Kentucky sent a delegation to Missouri, who were entrusted with the sacred charge of bringing back the remains of the great Hunter and his wife to the soil of the State that now delighted to honor him. Kentucky did not forget the services of Daniel Boone, and she determined that his bones should be kept nowhere but in her own soil. She resolved that he should repose, by the side of his devoted wife still, in the cemetery at Frankfort, where visitors from all parts of the country and the world might behold the resting-place of the great Pioneer. The removal of the bodies was effected with little trouble and perfect safety.

The ceremonies of the re-interment took place at Frankfort, on the 15th day of September, 1845. All Kentucky crowded to witness the memorable sight. It was something for a man to say even that he had seen the case containing the remains of Daniel Boone. He, the Pioneer, had come back among them again, having burst the cerements of the grave! Once more he walked the earth! Thousands and tens of thousands felt their hearts thrill with such a joy as they never before experienced, when these canonized bones were carried along in their presence. The most distinguished of Kentucky's sons were the pall-bearers on this occasion, who thus sincerely attested the deep reverence his great name had inspired in their hearts.

John J. Crittenden spoke the funeral oration,

which was eloquent and worthy of the occasion; himself the son of an early emigrant to Kentucky, and one of the foremost of American men. The funeral pageant was imposing in the extreme. No such gathering had before been seen in the limits of gallant Kentucky.

A fitting close to the story of this man of pure life, simple habits, unsullied honesty, and heroic endeavor. No shadow rests on the fame of Daniel Boone. He was all that could be asked as a father and a husband, and in all the relations he held toward others he was an exemplar. The day shone clear through his character. Nature does not produce such a man in every generation, or even in every century; when she does, it is with a specific purpose, which is always accomplished.

The ages will pronounce the name of Daniel Boone with pride. He was a true man. He was direct and self-reliant. There was no falsehood about his nature, and no need of any. He did great deeds as other men would do smaller ones, because the power lay in him to do them, and he could not help it. Though he never made any profession of religion before the public, it cannot be denied that he was the most thoroughly religious man that ever lived. It could not well be otherwise, for he drank in his inspiration direct from the fount of Nature, and that is ever as clean and pure as the waters that rill from the mountain. His sense of justice was ever untainted. No wrong could be laid at his door, and he passed away with only the blessings of the race upon his silvered head.

Let his name be honored forever.

www.ingramcontent.com/pod-product-compliance
Lightning Source LLC
Chambersburg PA
CBHW011950150426
43195CB00018B/2878